Richard David Rosenblatt

Maximilian Books

On Borrowed Time

V3.0 R1.0

Paperback ISBN: 978-0-578-18968-0
Hardback ISBN: 978-0-578-18969-7

Library of Congress Control Number: 2017933157

Maximilian Books

PRINTED IN THE UNITED STATES OF AMERICA

This book is dedicated to my best friend and wife, Lois.
She is the companion of my life,
and the champion of all my creative works.

I also want to express my gratitude to Garrett Chaffin-Quiray for his expert advice and for his encouragement.

Other books by Richard David Rosenblatt
BLACK GOLD GRAY 978-1-4327-1920-3
Co-authored with George Crall.

Table of Contents

Preface

The only benefit of advanced age is that one becomes the repository of a million scenes and stories.

Imagine that you saw, as I did as a child, Civil War Veterans marching to patriotic band music up New York's Fifth Avenue. Picture the venerable Grand Army of the Republic in their flashy blues, swords glinting in the sun, mingling with stately Confederate Veterans in their elegant gray with large hats topped in feathers.

Dinner at the Wings Club at the Biltmore in New York City at a round table with Eddie Rickenbacker and Jimmie Doolittle. Lunch with Albert Einstein. Tea with Eleanor Roosevelt. Lauren Bacall, The Sultan of Morocco, The Duke of Windsor, Salvador Dali, Marc Chagall, Jackson Pollock, and Kurt Weill.

In my life I've met the rulers of Russia, Spain, France, Morocco, the United States, and other leaders from around the world. I've known movie stars and moguls; captains of industry, the world's greatest scientists, famous generals, explorers, athletes, crooks, gamblers, and sociopaths. These short memoirs I pass on to you, the reader, in hope that they will inform and delight you.

CHAPTER 1

Poil de Carotte, 1932

IN 1932, HERBERT Hoover was President of the United States, Adolph Hitler wasn't yet Chancellor of Germany, and the South of France along the Mediterranean was sparsely populated because air conditioning wasn't yet part of everyday life.

That September our little family, including my parents, my brother, Rob, and our governess, Fraulein Richard, moved into the Hotel Westminster in Nice, on the Promenade des Anglais, the promenade of the English. This carefully plotted, wide road, with palms running along the center island of the four-lane avenue, served as the center of all our activities.

Confronting the Westminster was a beach consisting of stones the shape of flattened eggs. One had to wear rubber shoes when swimming in order to avoid climbing out of the water onto burning stones heated by the sun. Yet, for hundreds of years, visitors have found these same stones uniquely attractive. We children searched among them for small bits of smooth, clear-colored pebbles that had once been ancient Roman and Greek glass mosaics.

Rob and I didn't see much of our parents during our stay at the Westminster. In the evenings we ate with Fraulein Richard, either in the apartment, served by the waiters, or downstairs in the nearly empty, elegant, hotel restaurant. Children weren't then allowed in the hotel dining halls at night. This meant that we caught sight of our parents only in brief moments each evening as they left for gala parties or for trips to casinos up and down the Mediterranean coast.

These private casinos were furnished in the new fad of art deco and provided excellent food and music with the most famous entertainers in the world. The dancing included waltzes, tangos, fox trot, and rumba. The tango was so popular that some ladies dressed in seductive clothes with sequins and skirts slit up the sides to make them look like natives of Buenos Aires. To accentuate the provocative style, they added dark eye shadow, blood red lipstick, rouge, and cut their hair severely with a single provocative spit curl in front of each ear.

My mother wore gold lamé, white fur, and sometimes ostrich feathers; my father wore top hat, tails, and a white scarf. They had a chauffeur-driven open Bugatti, and looked like the King and Queen of a Balkan country driving off to a fabulous event like the Ballet Russe de Monte Carlo in the Royal castle of the Grimaldis in Monaco, or else to a soirée at the home of the painter Marc Chagall in nearby Grasse.

During the day Rob and I went to school at the Cours de Moulin, a boys grammar school, in a private mansion on the south end of the Promenade des Anglais. There were a few German boys, two Egyptians who spoke English, and scattered others, mostly French. We were the only Americans in the school where discipline was fast and harsh. No language, other than French, was permitted. We once tried speaking German and had our knuckles painfully rapped for the effort.

During recess in the back garden, we were allowed considerable freedom and permitted to wage murderous pitched battles with wooden swords and wooden shields. We divided into the ancient forces of Vercingetorix and Caesar, and fought those battles until the clanging bell called us back to classes. It was during one of these battles that I first heard insulting remarks about my hair, which was flaming red. An older boy picked me out with his sword and struck my shield, saying, "Take this, *poil de carotte*," meaning carrot head.

In those days, there were almost no redheads in France. This led French kids to adopt all sorts of bizarre views about "carrot tops," which also meant I was bullied and called "ginger," and forced to listen to stories about historic redheads who were evil, oversexed, and ill-tempered mutants. Redheads were, according to European legends that I soon learned, vampires, werewolves, and witches, and should be stamped out.

One gory story, in particular, stemmed from the alchemy of the middle ages and required blood from a red-haired boy in order to turn copper into gold. Even in England "gingerphobia" had reached its peak with red-haired women being stabbed as sexual temptresses, and young alienated red-haired boys committing suicide after vigorous torments.

At school one day, a particularly big, fat, dark-haired bully of a boy from Lyon told me that Christ was killed because he was a redhead. I knew from studying the Bible that Esau had been covered with red hair, and Mary Magdalene had long red hair, too, but to be crucified for a small genetic mutation was just off the wall. At the same time we were studying Homer's Iliad in Latin, an almost insurmountable task for a six-year-old American boy. The whole class read aloud that Achilles's bad temper came from the fact he was a redhead.

My isolation was complete.

It was also disturbing that I had no red-haired relatives. Not one in the whole family, both sides. My father said that we were descended from the Biblical King David who was a redhead but that seemed too far off to matter.

At that same time an award-winning French movie appeared. *Poil de Carotte* was the sad story of a boy born to French parents and cursed with red hair. He lived a wretched life, rejected by his peers and his family, especially by his mother, who all regarded him as an embarrassment and a useless oddity. The boy decided on suicide. "No one will miss me," he said, the poor poil de carotte. All France was in tears.

As for me, there was no sympathy, merely wonder. As a direct result of the movie, everywhere I went people pointed and said, "Poil de carotte, poil de carotte." My mother bought me a leather headgear, like a World War I pilot's head cover. I wore it for a while but my red eyebrows, eyelashes, and white freckled skin gave me away.

From my position, the times were a perfect storm of disquiet. The most popular movie in France was about a redheaded boy, and I was the only redheaded boy in France. Hotel maids gathered in my room at the Westminster, giggled, and tried to lift my bathrobe to see what the rest of me looked like. The elevator man announced loudly to strangers upon my entering his elevator: "Voila poil de carotte." On the front terrace waiters pointed me out to tables full of curious guests: "Poil de carotte." Doormen opened the door with a mock flourish reserved for royalty. "Monsieur Poil de Carotte." A man delivering a basket of long baguettes by bicycle shouted: "Aha, poil de carotte." And an elegant old lady dressed in black with a giant long pearl necklace peered at me with glasses attached to a chain around her neck. She said in a high falsetto, *"C'est domage qu'il n'est pas une fille"* (It's too bad he's not a girl).

I decided to face the issue and had a talk with Fraulein Richard. She was an attractive German woman in her late twenties from the northern port town of Bremen. She was a good soul, sincere and long suffering, in charge of two irascible, unpredictable, and sometimes dangerous boys, and I confided in her my deepest troubles.

How should I understand my French redhead dilemma and what was the movie *Poil de Carotte* all about? She replied that she would look into it and on her day off she went to see the movie.

The picture moved her so much that she couldn't report it to me without crying. She held my hand and told me about this poor boy, Francois, whose red hair ruined him. She turned and said to me in her native German: *"Du arme kind, du arme kind"* (You poor boy, you poor boy). I was now, to her, Francois, poil de carotte.

From that moment on Fraulein Richard regarded me as the most tragic soul she had ever known. This persisted for years. Sometimes she would comb my red hair and I would look at her, and her eyes would well up.

I knew just what she was thinking.

CHAPTER 2

Journey to Sheherazade, 1933

IN A SHEIK'S palace overlooking the Mediterranean, an ivory-skinned, black-haired woman dressed in a flowing paisley negligee sat on a soft couch and looked deep into my eyes. She had been reading to me from *Arabian Nights* while I sat on a giant pillow drinking in the surroundings.

"Dickie, you will remember these nights long after I am gone," she said.

It was 1933 and we were in an elegant palace on Mount Carmel in Haifa in the British Mandate of Palestine. The mysterious woman was my Aunt Madeleine, married to Major Fredric Partridge, head of the Palestine Constabulary, the British military police assigned to keep order in that part of the Middle East.

The palace was built in a circle with all the rooms surrounding a star-shaped reflecting pool and fountain. Servants moved from one room to another, robed in white. One trusted older man wore a turban. He had come with the Partridges from India.

To me Aunt Madeleine was Sheherazade, the heroine of "1,001 Arabian Nights" and one of only a handful of women seen as heroic in Middle Eastern culture, and it was no accident that she was reading to me from a brilliantly illustrated, recent translation of that famous Persian book. According to legend, King Shariar, ruler of Samarkand, discovered that his wife had been unfaithful and, as punishment, he had her killed, along with putting to death 3,000 virgins, one per day, as a warning to all women.

Before being put to death, Sheherazade offered to tell Shariar a story. He agreed and she kept him spellbound through the night, promising him more the following evening if he would wait. In this way she stopped the executions and began the 1,001 nights, about which she spun more and more interesting, and exciting, tales for a bloodthirsty king who eventually stayed all scheduled executions and made Sheherazade his queen.

I sat there in my aunt's vast bedroom, lit only by candles, listening to her read these stories, my latter day Sheherazade, and the air burned with incense to repel mosquitoes. We drank tea from the little bronze cups served from a samovar and I retraced the steps I'd taken to end up in Aunt Madeleine's chamber.

The year was 1931 and we were scheduled to go to Europe for the summer. At the last minute, my mother received a letter from her older sister, Madeleine Partridge, which explained that Aunt Madeleine was ill. We immediately changed our plans and headed for Alexandria, Egypt, the nearest reachable port to Haifa where Aunt Madeleine and Uncle Fred lived.

The journey to Alexandria would take 25 days aboard the American Export Line's Exeter and it would stop at several ports across the Mediterranean. My father stayed behind in order to close some business dealings but our little family made a good team. Mother led the way, as in all things, followed closely by my brother Rob and me, and our governess, Fraulein Gertrude Richard. The ship pulled out of New York harbor, passed the Statue of Liberty, Ellis Island, and the Narrows, and then pushed on towards the vast Atlantic Ocean.

In those years ships were not as grand and comfortable as they are today. Except for a few great ocean liners, most were like the Exeter, just ordinary steamers carrying passengers and cargo to ports all over the world.

The Exeter had been newly built and was on its maiden voyage to the Mediterranean. The American Export Line had just commenced passenger service on merchant ships, expanding operations from 12 to 125 passengers per ship, so our experience was unprecedented.

By 1942 the Exeter entered wartime service with the US Navy as a transport ship and was renamed the USS Edward Rutledge. It was torpedoed that same year by the German submarine, U-130, and went down off the coast of Casablanca, Morocco.

Because the Exeter had been built before the invention of stabilizers, it tossed on the sea like a toy plastic duck in a wavy bathtub. Passengers were often at the railings, tossing up carefully served meals. The power of suggestion and smell spread the seasickness among normally steady passengers so each day's journey was a test of patience and intestinal fortitude.

One day Robbie, my older brother, and I were in a devilish mood. We enjoyed a big breakfast, somehow remaining immune to seasickness, and then went on deck to describe, with relish, to one and all, each and every dish we had consumed, setting off another round of seasickness among passengers.

Despite the occasional roughness of the trip, life onboard consisted of ritualistic meal times and other social appearances where status was a matter of great importance, even to those who normally took that sort of thing for granted. Dignified clothing, lustrous jewelry, and the location of one's table nearest the Captain marked one's relative standing. Even the attending governesses basked in the reflected glory of their employers' esteem, enjoying gossip, some of which was nothing but jealous invention.

Unlike today, children were not to be seen or heard, except for some weekly turnouts during the cruise. Over the 25-day trip there were four such command performances where we children were required to appear at a makeshift theater and perform the poems, dances, or songs we had learned during the previous week. Mother had us deliver our contributions in German and French, which we prepared so well I still remember some of the poems today.

Children also did not eat meals with their parents; nor did children enter lounges, bars, or card rooms. There was a separate children's dining room furnished with small tables and chairs, and most children stayed in staterooms attached to the parental room by a central living area. This division among passengers supported an entirely separate world of children aboard the Exeter. In our community governesses usually wore starched white nurse uniforms but acted like army sergeants and were strict enforcers of table etiquette and the "clean plate" dictum.

One strange lapse in adult supervision was the habit of putting bottles of wine on each table in the children's dining room. Due to such invitation, one day when Fraulein Richard stayed on deck with seasickness, Robbie and I drank half a bottle of wine, got properly tipsy, and were ejected from the dining room.

In spite of all the furnished luxury, though, pipes and painted-over rivets were evident in all rooms that had only small round portholes for windows. Heavy step-over bulkheads led into the bathrooms, which were spare and often troubled by smelly pump contraptions that were sometimes out of service.

For our amusement there was a gymnasium that featured a vibrating band that was put around a person's middle to tighten the waistline. Another machine moved like a horse and another moved like a camel. Rob and I watched in horror as a big fat Turkish gentleman, with a towel around his neck, fell off the camel machine. "I haff never been on a camel before," he exclaimed apologetically.

On deck there were quoits, or a rope fashioned into a small hoop to be thrown on a peg, like horseshoes. There was also shuffleboard, and trapshooting off the stern of the ship.

All around the ship was an enclosed wood deck. It was used constantly, except at lunch and dinner, and was the main exercise and social activity for everyone. Dressing for a morning stroll could put one in mind of the elegance required on New York's Fifth Avenue come Easter Sunday.

Also along this promenade were numerous deck chairs where women reclined, tucked in by attentive stewards, to read books or talk, while the men marched around at a quick pace, brandishing canes for show, and wearing overcoats with spats over their shoes. The glassed-in deck could be cold in the North Atlantic so at 11 AM hot bouillon was served with a plain Saltine cracker to guests in the deck chairs.

Lunch was in the dining hall and it was a dressy affair. Meals were laid out in several courses and there was an ever-present string quartet accompanied by a pianist, the five players offering light operetta music and gypsy-type string arrangements. Because dancing at lunch was discouraged, music was carefully selected not to provoke and when the meal was done, passengers retired to their cabins to rest up for tea, which was another major social event.

Women wore hats or bandanas. Art deco costume jewelry was in vogue with large pieces festooning ear lobes and fingers, sometimes with original modern designs done up in rhinestone. Men wore jackets and colorful vests, and almost always carried a cane, waving them as thought they were swords.

Tea was held in the Grand Salon where the string quartet and pianist were fortified by saxophone and drums. A dance floor was cleared and a long table was covered with trays of little triangular cucumber sandwiches with crusts carefully trimmed and then echeloned around each tray next to platters of plain-tasting sugar cookies. Waiters moved around the tables wearing white gloves, handing out plates and serving the sandwiches and cookies with small silver pincers.

Aside from waltzes, and the new fox trot, the two-step and polka were popular. The most popular dance, though, was the tango. The tangos of those times were much less athletic than the current style. Some people danced while hardly moving, their bodies pressed together and moving in suggestive back and forth patterns that raised a few eyebrows.

After tea was finished, an exhausted dancer might retire to their cabin to rest up for dinner while others continued their march around deck. Card players plowed on to the card room where bridge was the serious game, although poker was considered more sporting. Usually each trip included professional card sharks and whenever we travelled with Father he always talked with the officer in charge of the card room to find out which players to avoid. Mother found the whole habit disagreeable, saying that all gambling was a waste of time and money. Instead she spent her time reading, writing poetry, and sketching drawings for future paintings.

To occupy my time on board I had schoolbooks, piano lessons, and poems to memorize. Robbie had the same responsibilities, along with keeping up his violin lessons. Sometimes we practiced together but the sounds of our rehearsals were so awful we were usually asked to go elsewhere.

On that trip I made new friends. One was a mysterious Indian Maharajah who wore a magnificent giant ruby in his turban. He had a great dark cape and wore heavy leather sandals covered with baggy pants. He spoke to me kindly in a distinctly British accent and I introduced him to my mother with whom he developed an instant rapport and so insisted on accompanying her to dinner. "He is a perfect gentleman," she said, whatever that meant.

The young governesses, meanwhile, had the pick of the crew for romantic intrigues, and sometimes the pick of the passengers, too. Furtive relationships were more obvious than they imagined, and of course little children weren't supposed to know, but they did.

When we pulled into Gibraltar the morning was crystal-clear. A single great stone covered with hundreds of monkeys rose like a mountain from the ocean's surface. British officers dressed in pith helmets and khaki shorts, and carrying leather swagger sticks, climbed out of a motor launch. They worked their way up a wood and rope ladder on the side of the ship and onto the deck where they were received by virtually all the passengers that stood at the railings to watch the little ceremony of the ship's officers accepting the right of inspection.

Refueling lines were attached to the ship and some boxes were offloaded onto barges, by a winch, from deep in the ships holds. "Smoking is prohibited while refueling is in progress," announced the loudspeaker, which immediately brought to light the prospect of a ship on fire, an extraordinary joy to little boys. We discussed this possibility at length. Lunch was served in the dining rooms, as usual, and the ship moved on, headed for Marseilles, France, our first stop in the shimmering aquamarine Mediterranean.

Two days later, as we sailed through quiet waters off the coast of southern France, the silence was broken by announcements over the loudspeaker that those landing and leaving the ship at Marseilles must have their bags tagged and placed outside their cabins so stevedores could pick them up. Passports and visas were necessary and all were given careful instruction to settle ship bills with the purser.

As we approached the harbor, there were boys in the water. Passengers leaned over the ship's railing and tossed coins to the boys who dove underwater to get them. This seemed to me costly and pointless but it was apparently a ritual consistently observed aboard ship whenever arriving at port.

We went on shore for a few hours to visit Marseilles, the oldest city in France. The maharajah came along, lending an air of mystery to our expedition. The ship was not to leave until morning so at our leisure we rode a horse drawn carriage, and stopped at a seafood restaurant on the edge of the port. The local specialty was bouillabaisse, a soup filled with local fish and laced with a buttery cream containing fennel, olive oil, saffron, onion, tomatoes, and other secrets of the chef. I saved some celery and squares of sugar for our carriage horse.

Afterward, we moved on to the Palais de Longchamps, a big wedding cake of a structure with columns everywhere and an Italianesque fountain cascading to a lower level. We passed a high hill butting into the bay with an unusual cathedral, Notre Dame de la Garde, topped by a huge, thin spire with a statue that looked like a finger pointing accusingly at heaven. Out in the bay we saw the island of If, pronounced, "eef," and the Chateau d'If that formed the basis of Alexander Dumas's book *The Count of Monte Cristo*.

We sailed off from Marseilles, on our way to Genoa and Naples, in southern Italy. Life on board resumed its routine tedium, except for some readjustment resulting from the departure of passengers and the arrival of new ones, and the food took on a Mediterranean flavor due to the provisions taken on board in Marseilles.

Elegant little menus were placed on each table announcing dishes with familiar French and Italian Riviera location names, such as *Fruits de Mer Monte Carlo*, meaning "seafood cocktail," or *Spaghetti San Remo* and *Gallantine de Veau Vesuvius*. None of these dishes can be found in the *Encyclopedia of European Cooking* since they were all made up for the occasion but the little menus were covered with attractive color paintings of familiar European destinations, such as a flower stall at the foot of the Eiffel Tower, sailboats in a rough sea off the Rock of Gibraltar, and book stalls outside the Coliseum in Rome. Passengers were urged to keep these menus as mementos of this once-in-a-lifetime voyage, and so we did.

At Genoa, to our surprise, we were not permitted ashore. Cargo was off-loaded by crane while a small group of vendors were allowed on-board. They sold cameo broaches, lace, fans, oversize beads, local postcards, and little boxes with small spy holes which, when held to the eye, showed black-and-white views of buxom French ladies in their birthday suits.

A dozen passengers debarked with their steamer trunks and a collection of heavy leather valises held together with great leather straps. All the trunks and bags were festooned with 5x4 inch, glued-on advertisements for hotels and shipping lines from all over the world. Pasted on haphazardly as people left hotels and ships, the advertisements provided a final, non-removable testimony to the fact that a traveler had indeed been to somewhere unusual. Cumulatively, these ads were badges of honor, not unlike military campaign ribbons and medals. They were silent, but colorful, proof of a well-seasoned traveler and those without pasted luggage were regarded as greenhorns or nouveau riches, and were consequently easy marks for card sharks, swindlers, and panhandlers.

A day later, we pulled into Naples, passing the romantic Isle of Capri at the mouth of the bay with Mount Vesuvius spouting smoke in the distance. As the Exeter approached the mooring, a mournful brass band played what sounded like a funeral dirge led by a great, dented brass tuba wrapped around a fat little man no larger that his instrument. The band was dressed in faded white uniforms with gold epaulettes, as though they were leftover generals from the Great War. Boys once again surrounded the ship, diving for coins.

Mother had arranged a busy two days while the ship was re-supplied. Our immediate destination was the volcano Vesuvius so we entered a big black limousine with an Italian guide wearing an official-looking cap with a visor badge from American Express. His English was miserable but Mother knew some Italian so we made do. The guide took a shine to Fraulein Richard, who was immediately annoyed at his attentions as we drove up part of the mountain, got out, and climbed to where there was grey-colored lava. Rob and I climbed down an old crater where sulphur escaped from a hole in the ground. We gasped and covered our mouths with handkerchiefs, and later learned that the volcano erupted without notice a few days afterward, pouring live red-hot lava down the mountain toward Pompeii.

We, too, visited Pompeii and saw the amazing results of that famous ancient eruption. Life had been perfectly preserved as it was in Roman times when the ash suddenly descended, burying everything and everyone and creating permanent molds from which castings were poured. Evidence of life was preserved just as it was that very minute of the eruption. The white plaster models with horrified expressions were lying about in the act of running or hiding

There was also a pornographic statue of a man that so outraged Fraulein that she turned the two of us around. I didn't understand it, then, but Robbie said he did. There were rooms with lurid paintings in them; but they were "not open to women and children."

The next day we took a launch that sailed to the island of Capri where we mounted a donkey-drawn carriage for a tour of the island. We returned to the dock and entered a rowboat that arrived at the entrance to the Blue Grotto in full sunlight, but in rough sea waves. We had to lie down while our boat slipped under the low cave entrance. Inside, there was a most amazing, luminous, sapphire glow caused by sunlight bouncing off white sand at the bottom of the sea and reflecting upwards into the grotto. Another boat followed us, bobbing up and down while some worried Italian women shouted prayers and crossed themselves.

That night we left for the port city of Piraeus, outside Athens, in Greece. This was a dull place, made worse by a driving rain. Our carriage tour was shortened when Mother said it was cruel for horses to be worked in such bad weather.

The Exeter arrived in Alexandria, Egypt, at night. There was no berth for our ship so we disembarked along floating pontoons strung together to shore while bearers brought along our steamer trunks and bags under the glow of bare light bulbs strung above the bobbing pontoons.

A few hours later we entered a private first-class car in an old railroad train that ran slowly to Cairo. The train stopped at a lonely spot in the desert where the steam engine took on water. Fraulein went out and filled a small jar with sand from the desert and it was more like talcum powder than like beach sand.

Near midnight we arrived at the ancient railroad station in Cairo. Uncle Fred was there to meet us. He wore an impressive uniform with brown boots and his khaki dress tunic, topped with a crown on his shoulders, the rank of British major.

He brought up his two-door Ford with an open rumble seat in back. There was also a little truck for the luggage, driven by Uncle Fred's bodyguard, a Turkish sergeant from the Palestine constabulary who was dressed all in black, from his boots to a tall lamb's wool military hat.

We drove, Uncle Fred at the wheel, Mother and Fraulein on the front seat, and Rob and I in the rear rumble seat. When we reached the Suez Canal, the cars drove onto Uncle Fred's barge and native men dressed in cotton skirts pulled a rope to move us across the locks.

We rode the rest of the night and well into the next day until we reached Haifa along the coast road. Once during the night, I went to sleep and nearly fell out of the rumble seat but Rob grabbed me by the pants and pulled me in.

Finally, in the morning air on the steps of the palace on Mount Carmel, we'd found Aunt Madeleine, my Sheherazade, who stood in her flowing paisley negligee, waiting to hug and squeeze me.

CHAPTER **3**

The Stowaway, 1933

Aboard the S.S. Exeter

IN ANCIENT TIMES, Marsala, now known as Marseilles, was a place to which unsavory Greeks were exiled. Sufficiently far away from Greece, it was assumed that only someone with the determination of Ulysses could ever work his way back to what the Greeks called "civilization."

The Marseilles stevedore climbed up the gangplank onto the ship. He thrust my big leather bag under my bunk, screamed, and withdrew a bloody arm.

It was 1933 and Marseilles was then the largest port in the Mediterranean but it was populated by the human flotsam left over from the Great War. Along its streets, some men, called *les geuls casés*, the broken faces, wore masks to hide their injuries.

Our stevedore was an able-bodied war veteran, tall and hairy, and he looked tough enough to wrestle a lion. He wore a royal blue smock and carried a great leather belt he could string through a number of bags in order to carry the whole bunch at one time. He spoke in grunts and was nobody you wanted to challenge.

My mother was in charge of our traveling group, which consisted of my older brother, Rob, our governess Fraulein Richard, me, and a certain little black Scottish Terrier named Paddy.

In those years, Scotties were very popular. Recently elected, President Franklin Roosevelt had a similar black Scottie named Fala, who managed to get into the news more often than his owners wished.

Once, it was alleged that a presidential boat had been dispatched to bring the dog somewhere, and the dreaded newspaper columnist Westbrook Pegler wrote a scalding piece about what a shame this was, in the middle of the Depression, a waste of expensive resources, and all that. Not to be outdone, our President, in one of his enchanting "Fireside Chats," said something like, "You can criticize me, you can criticize Eleanor, you can even criticize my sons, but when you criticize my little dog Fala, he doesn't like it."

We had been driven down to the port of Marseilles from our hotel in Nice, higher up on the Riviera. We rode in the hotel's black, box-shaped Rolls Royce with 19 pieces of luggage piled on top, and covered by a great black tarp. My mother carried Paddy the Scottie over her arm, as we were unloaded from the Rolls.

In those days dogs were not allowed on ships. This was strict and immutable, no exceptions. My mother knew this. But it never stopped her from taking exception. Yet she was also shrewd enough to know that her argument would never impress an "old salt" captain so she adopted a winning deception that never failed.

She would carry the dog over her arm and cover it with a blanket. This blanket, called a "rug," was an ever-present traveling necessity. Cars did not have heaters and often neither did waiting rooms or hotels, so with a rug we marched onto ships all over the world with Paddy, always silent, draped under my mother's arm inside the rug. Once onboard ship, Paddy was carefully hidden under my bunk, way back, knowing somehow that his life depended on him staying there in silence.

After a day or two, my mother would insist on seeing the ship's captain. She'd then announce, in her most innocent voice, that she had a dog and was completely unaware of a rule that dogs were not permitted onboard. The problem was now neatly shifted to the captain, whether to throw the dog overboard or allow a one-time transgression. The gambit never failed. She had unfortunately pulled this act on this ship two years earlier, but fortunately, this wasn't the same captain.

Following a strict lecture, including a reminder that he could have easily thrown the dog into the ocean, but that he was, nevertheless, a soft-hearted guy, this one time violation would be allowed, but never again. My mother acted accordingly, and allowed that she had learned her lesson, and would never again carry a dog onto a ship.

On this particular day, the stevedore had thrust my bag into Paddy, who had been hiding under my bunk, and that was too much, even for a well-behaved Scottie. He took one great bite out of this tough stevedore and all hell broke loose.

The terrible scream was heard in my mother's cabin on the other side of the adjoining living room and she rushed in, followed by the governess and my brother. The stevedore let out with curses known only to war veterans and toilette attendants. His arm dripped blood. The governess blanched and sat down to keep from fainting. My brother and I looked on, fascinated.

My mother, who was up to every occasion, retrieved her medical kit that she carried everywhere. Her medical training had taken place in 1915 while traveling with her family from New York to San Diego to see the Pan American Exposition when their train derailed in Arizona. Two hundred people were injured and there were no doctors, so my aunt, Madeleine, who had been a nurse in the trenches of France in 1914, and who had her medical case, took action with my mother as nurse's assistant. Forty-eight hours later, my mother had become so adept that her sister gave her the medical kit.

My mother opened the kit and applied a tourniquet while cleaning and sterilizing the stevedore's wound. At the same time she kept up a running set of assurances, all in French, that things would be fine, that the stevedore would be satisfied with his coming settlement.

"Je vais mourir" (I will die), he moaned, until, finally, his arm was bandaged with more gauze than needed, making it look like a great white bundle.

Out of my mother's purse came a thick roll of French francs. She stuffed these large paper bills into the man's hands and said, *"Cent, deux cents, trois cents, quatre cents. Ça soufié?"* (One hundred, two hundred, three hundred, four hundred. Is that enough?) Mother was thinking about how this could escalate into an international incident. The dog would be found, we would be charged with causing great harm to a war veteran, and we would be held in prison in Marseilles incommunicado.

He picked up the rhythm. "*Non, non, je vais mourir*" (No, no, I'm going to die).

More hundreds were counted out, followed by more "Non, non." Eventually, it was settled and the man left.

Later we stood at the rails as the ship pulled out of Marseilles. All the stevedores on the pier were required to wave as the ship maneuvered past the docks. There on the pier, amongst them, was a waving arm with a great white bandage.

CHAPTER 4

The Bicycle, 1935

CROSS THE RIVER over an old trestle bridge and you're in New Hope, PA, home of the Broadway summer art colony in 1935. Turn right off the bridge and you are on Main Street, passing the summer rental homes of famous actors, writers, and composers. On the left you pass the wooden balconied house of Kurt Weill, composer of "The Threepenney Opera" and "Lady in the Dark," and the motion picture *One Touch of Venus* starring Rita Hayworth. His wife, Lotte Lenya, was often seen sitting on an old rocking chair.

Drive on beyond the Weill house, and Main Street curves left over a bridge across the barge canal before curving right into the Amish country farms with their black horse and carriages. At that right-hand curve is an old dirt road climbing up a hill to a white clapboard house surrounded by a bright green grass lawn, circled with pink peonies nestled in coral rhododendrons.

We spent the summer of 1935 in that white house on the hill. I was 9 and my father was financing the Broadway production of the musical "The Eternal Road," produced by the great Max Reinhardt with book by Franz Werfel, and music by Kurt Weill.

Every day I rode my bicycle from the white house on the hill, down the dirt entry road, past the canal and onto Main Street, and to the wooden front porch of the Weill house. In the large living room was a grand piano, and on the left, an old loom. Lotte taught me to weave things on the loom while Kurt composed on the piano, using a nubby pencil and a pad of lined music paper.

This went on all summer, with one noteworthy exception.

One morning, riding down from the house on the dirt road at full speed, I came upon the mailman driving his old box-shaped, Model T Ford up the dirt driveway. My brakes couldn't stop the bike and I crashed into the Ford, head on, and flew off the bike onto the hood of the car, through the windshield, and into the chest of the mailman. I went out like a light but awakened on the couch of the white house back on the hill. The mailman was unhurt and I recovered quickly but the bike was mangled beyond repair.

In a few days, my parents gave me a brand new bicycle, a gleaming Cadillac of a bike, with bells and whistles, and a rear red reflector that looked like the biggest ruby in the world. I resumed my visits to the loom, Kurt, and Lotte.

A week later, my new bicycle was stolen from the porch of the Weill house. I came out in the late afternoon for my return trip home and it was gone.

I was furious and I acted badly. A spoiled brat who never did anything to deserve a beautiful new bike; I was inconsolable. Kurt and Lotte begged me to be philosophic about the loss and assured me that it would be found, somehow. The police department of New Hope was notified to aid in the bike's recovery.

The next day the bicycle was found and the thief caught. He was a thin, sad-looking boy about my age. He wore a dirty shirt over tight knickers and one sock covered one leg while the other encircled his shoe. A poor kid from the tin roofed shacks that lined the railroad tracks, he was brought to the Weill house where I was summoned to sign a complaint by a patrolman in shiny strap boots.

The law would be followed to the letter and the boy would receive whatever punishment the local judge would feel was justified. With that I was satisfied and ready to sign the complaint.

Kurt Weill took me aside and asked me if he could speak with me. This man who was a towering musical giant and a victim of intolerance and cruelty in his native Germany, and who expressed in his music his love of compassion and kindness, was requesting an audience with me to discuss the theft of a bicycle.

He told me that he had inquired about the boy-thief and learned that his mother was dead and that his father hadn't found work during the whole Depression. The boy didn't have a bike of his own and he had seen my shiny new bicycle on the steps of the Weill house. All he wanted was to know what it would be like to ride such a beautiful bike.

"Just imagine you were that boy," Kurt said.

I dropped my complaint. No charges were ever filed.

CHAPTER 5

Relativity, 1936

ALBERT EINSTEIN WAS my father. This confusing idea entered my head at an early age. For starters he was an old family friend who visited us at home and we occasionally went for lunch on Sundays to that house of his on Mercer Street in Princeton. But my real suspicions took root from the fact that my mother often visited him, alone, motoring in from Manhattan in our Buick limousine, separated from our Scandinavian chauffeur by a glass window which went up and down with a button, controlled from the rear.

One Sunday, my whole family drove to Princeton in that Buick and we spotted Einstein heading away from his house, dressed carelessly in a gray sweatshirt and pants, wearing tennis shoes and no socks. He was walking briskly, his eyes looking straight forward, apparently focused on nothing.

My father called out, "Hello professor."

Einstein instantly snapped out of whatever trance he was in. "Hello, Willie." He spoke in a picturesque, heavy German accent punctuated with moments of silence and the gentle utterance, "ya," which I suspect was laid on a bit thick for his audience. "What are you doing here?"

"We are here to have lunch at your house."

"Oh." Einstein was confused but also seemed to me a jolly Santa Claus who would take me on his knee and bounce me. He reminded me of Heidi's grandfather who lived in the Swiss mountains.

We drove up to the Mercer Street house and were greeted by Mrs. Einstein.

"Albert will be home soon," Elsa said.

We entered the home and awaited the professor's arrival. I was dressed in some sort of little Lord Fauntleroy suit. It was black velvet with a white lace collar and buttons at the bottom of the pants. I would have been mortified if any of the boys at school saw me this way and felt I was too old for, "those beautiful golden curls," as my mother called them, and which tumbled down to my shoulders. I must have looked something like "The Infanta" or Gainsborough's "The Blue Boy."

Einstein entered the house and immediately hugged me. "My Eton boy," he said because my outfit bore some resemblance to the archaic costume of Eton College in England.

I blushed and thought about what he meant by "My Eton boy!" Where did that "my" come from?

I considered the question and remembered one of my mother's dinner parties where I was trotted out to meet all the guests and to talk with them briefly before I returned to my homework. I'd listened in on conversations to which I was not a party and in this way overheard one lady say that Einstein was a ladies' man and that his wife, who was also his cousin, didn't interfere with his affairs, provided she approved of the lady in question.

Putting two and two together, I realized that Albert Einstein addressed me with the possessive "my," that my mother was close to Mrs. Einstein, and that Mrs. Einstein no doubt approved of my mother. Ergo I was Einstein's illegitimate son.

On that Little Lord Fauntleroy day I captured the moment of this breathtaking truth by taking a picture of my mother lovingly surrounded by Elsa and Albert Einstein, my presumptive stepmother and biological father. I used my Kodak Brownie box camera and carried this secret guilt with me, and resulting picture, for a very long time.

It didn't help that I looked different from my brothers. People sometimes commented that I didn't look like anyone in my father's family. I could hardly confront my mother and Einstein was too involved in understanding the universe to deal with my problems of paternity and self-worth. There was even a story going around that he paid little enough attention to his legitimate children so there wasn't much hope that he'd acknowledge me as his own.

I even saw in the newspapers an account of a man, also named Einstein, who wrote in German to the professor. "I may be related to you, Doctor Einstein. Can you tell me if that is, indeed, so?"

The man received no reply so he wrote another letter. "I am really troubled. Are we related?"

This time the man got a reply from Einstein that was written across the top of his letter. *Ihre sorgen zol ich haben,* the professor wrote, meaning, literally, "Your troubles I should have."

If this other possible relative couldn't get a straight answer, how could I?

CHAPTER **6**

Sex and the Small Child, 1936

MY BROTHER WAS charged with taking me to Central Park to sail my little sailboat but we ended up instead at the greatest topless show in New York. I was 10 years old. My brother, Rob, who was four years older than me, made a habit of dragging me to baseball games at Yankee Stadium or Giant's Polo Grounds. This time out on the town we would go down to Broadway and visit the fleshpots.

In those days four or five great movie theatres had first showings of the latest Hollywood pictures sandwiched in between vaudeville variety shows and performances by name bands like Tommy Dorsey, Cab Calloway, Glenn Miller and Benny Goodman. There were Hungarian acrobats, little white spotty dogs jumping through flaming hoops, and bedroom farces with old gents getting into ambiguous situations with chambermaids.

This day we were headed for Minsky's Burlesque. On the bus to school my brother had heard that there would be something worth seeing, although I didn't catch on to exactly what. But I did know there wasn't a prayer that two scruffy kids, one with a sailboat under his arm, would be allowed to enter this "adults only" show of shows, even with the price of entry.

Still, my brother dragged me around to the side street where the exit doors were just opening and shady-looking men in two-piece, un-pressed suits were leaving. As they pushed out the side-doors, we sneaked in and hid amongst the seats.

When the show started, we were right up front. This was the middle of the Great Depression and although most people would spend their money on food, the house was nearly full of men you'd never invite to dinner on Park Avenue. The band consisted of a pianist, a violinist who used his bow to lead, and a fat guy in shirtsleeves holding a big bass fiddle, the size of a fully-grown grizzly bear. In the corner was a drummer with all the equipment, including oversized cymbals.

The curtain went up and a man came out telling a long string of jokes to which the crowd snickered. None of it made sense to me. Next up was a bedroom scene where a well-dressed actor got his clothes off and had a set of pajamas underneath.

He gets into bed. A maid knocks on the door. He says, "Enter." The maid walks in and gets into bed. Someone else knocks, and the man shouts, "Oh my god, it's my wife." He climbs out of bed and dives underneath it. The door opens and it's not his wife but another man who gets into bed with the maid. Another knock on the door and the man under the covers yells, "Oh my god, it's my wife." The man in bed dives under the bed, and so on, until, after the last knock on the door, five men lie under the bed with the maid on top when the wife finally knocks and comes in. She sees the maid alone in bed and gives her hell for sleeping on the job and leaves. The men get out from under the bed and bow to the audience. The audience cheers.

Afterwards a line of chorus girls did a badly coordinated can-can showing the rear of their loose panties. More acts followed but finally we arrived at the main event.

"The star of our show, what you've all been waiting for," said the announcer. "PEACHES SOUTHERN and her world renowned SUN DANCE."

Claps and loud whistles filled the theater and out marched a large-bosomed blonde. Never mind that she was at least 40-years old, all her equipment was intact beneath a peach-colored bra that matched a peach-colored tutu. High heel shoes with straps wound up her legs suggesting Eve's friend the snake. The band came alive as the bumping and grinding increased into something more substantial.

Peaches grabbed the curtain and pulled it out to the middle of the stage. The band banged out "bump ta ta... bump ta ta... bump ta ta... bump." My brother and I sat on the edges of our seats. Then Peaches slipped off the tutu, revealing a tiny flower on her you-know-what. Off went the bra, and, as the finale, Peaches Southern made love to the edge of the curtain. It was the dramatic highlight of the show, of that afternoon, and of my life up to age 10.

When we got home to 1125 Park Avenue, with me still clutching the sailboat, Mother greeted us at the door. "Did you boys have a good time sailing your boat?"

"Wonderful," we said in unison.

CHAPTER 7

The Kindness of Strangers, 1936

I LOOKED UP and saw a giant Nazi swastika in the air above me. I walked out of Bloomingdales with my mother and the Hindenburg Zeppelin was making a triumphant flight over Central Park on its way to its mooring station in New Jersey. It was the height of the Great Depression and the streets were lined with out-of-work people. Some sold fruit and near the Bloomingdales entrance on Lexington Avenue, above the subway, a carefully groomed man in a three-piece suit tried to sell Irish linen handkerchiefs without success.

My mother had bought soap and toilet paper at Bloomingdales, which she ordered for delivery to our apartment on Park Avenue. Now we were going to Saks Fifth Avenue to buy me a suit.

On the way we stopped at Horn & Hardart, "The Automat," at 57th Street. My mother always kept a record sheet of my deportment and if I achieved a sufficient number of gold stars I was allowed to have my lunch at this restaurant of wonders where the walls were lined with food in little windows, perhaps five rows high. For three nickels dropped into a slot, a little window would pop open and a sandwich was yours for the taking. A salad in a little dish could be had from another window for five cents more. Hot dishes were 25 cents, and for another inserted nickel a boy could have hot chocolate or coffee poured out of a gold spout.

I made my choices, put money in the slots, and carried the plates to the cafeteria tables near the windows on 57th Street. I noticed unkempt men sitting at tables along the walls. They sat in a defensive posture and were badly dressed, not eating and obviously doing nothing. I watched them in wonder, and thought, what are those kind of people doing in this restaurant? I asked my mother about them but she didn't have any explanation.

As I looked on I saw that these men visited the spout marked by a sign that read, "Free hot water." Instead of being used for tea at five cents a bag, they poured the hot water into an empty mug and went back to their table where they mixed in free Heinz ketchup, and salt and pepper. Instant tomato soup! And all free!

I asked a man who was cleaning empty tables why Horn & Hardart would allow, "those bums," to use their restaurant as, "a flop house."

He replied: "It is the policy of the owners not to turn anyone away, no matter how unfortunate."

CHAPTER 8

The Last Flight of the Hannibal, 1936

A YEAR BEFORE Amelia Earhart was lost I flew from London to Paris. It was 1936 and at that time Britain had only one airline, Imperial Airways, which operated the airborne equivalent of the Orient Express. Each trip bore a certain resemblance to *Around the World in 80 Days*. Projected arrival times were wishful thinking and a variety of unexpected events was the order of the day over the course of a journey that commenced in London, stopping in Paris en route to Brindisi, Italy, then on to Athens, Cyprus, Alexandria, Baghdad, Karachi, Delphi, and, finally, arriving in Australia.

Six PM on the evening of July 31, 1936, we emerged from the Grosvenor House Hotel, opposite Hyde Park in London, and climbed into a box-shaped Rolls Royce limousine sent by Imperial Airways to collect us and our luggage for the motor trip to Croyden Airport. My mother attacked these adventures with the same Victorian precision and advance planning she devoted to a dinner party or a charitable affair. Twenty-one pieces of heavy leather luggage had been packed the day before, and in such a way that the loss of any one piece would not render any of us inoperative. Extra sets of underwear, shirts, and trousers were divided up among the bags and the 21 matched pieces were loaded, lovingly and artistically, onto the Rolls' rooftop before being covered with a shiny black tarpaulin. Mother taught us to, "never be separated from your luggage."

The six of us were packed into the plush interior with much the same ceremony. My father managed traveling with an austere detachment, leaving arrangements, instructions, and the handing out of monies to my mother. As an investment banker, he had a certain dignity to maintain. My mother entered next, clutching the usual extra blankets and coats and her medical kit—a necessity for one who travelled as far as she.

Next into the giant Rolls was my four-year old brother, Peter, accompanied by his governess, "Fraulein," as she was affectionately called. She was a tall, slim, craggy, aristocratic woman whose actual name was Eleanora von Schaumberg. Her father had been editor of a German newspaper when Hitler came to power, forcing her family to escape into Switzerland.

A well-educated, kindly, generous, and selfless person, Fraulein was living proof that there was another Germany during those terrible days when the world came to realize the horrors perpetrated by the Nazis. She was an inspiration to us all, as well, with her genuine enthusiasm for travel and learning, and for the relish with which she spoke English and French as well as German, all with the highest aristocratic accent.

She read to me continually: Jules Verne, when we were on the ocean liner *Normandie*, Charles Dickens while in England, and the other great classics when any opportunity arose. I can still remember her riding into London on the Boat Train from Southampton where the *Normandie* had docked, saying, "Fancy being in London."

The doorman at the Grosvenor took off his top hat, reached into the Rolls and set up the upright jump seats for my Cousin Freddy Partridge and me. From this vantage we enjoyed the best view out of the big square windows of the car.

Cousin Freddy, we called Fredic, was Aunt Madeleine's boy. After World War I she had gone to India and met Rudyard Kipling who introduced her to a British officer, Fred Partridge, who had been Lawrence of Arabia's senior officer during the first World War. Their son, Fredic, was exactly my age and he'd spent his earlier years in India, Egypt, and Palestine where his father commanded the Palestine Constabulary of the British Army.

Possibly as a result of our early introduction to flying this day, Cousin Fredic and I would both become pilots, he with the RAF and I with the U.S. Air Force. Ezer Weizman, Fredic's next door neighbor in Haifa, with whom he and I became friendly, also became a pilot with the RAF and eventually the head of the Israeli Air Force, in which his services were invaluable as the hero of the Six Day War. He later became President of Israel.

The big Rolls limo lumbered along Hyde Park, laden with baggage like an old stagecoach. We passed the point, where, a few days earlier, we had seen King Edward VIII shot at by a deranged assassin.

Mother and I had been riding horses on the bridle path when the royal entourage approached on horseback from the other direction. A man came up from the roadway, brandishing an old revolver, firing it into the air, and missing Edward. Although the royal household police caught him immediately, the event seems never to have appeared in English history books, although it was reported in the newspapers of the time. Not long afterwards, Edward abdicated to marry Wallis Warfield Simpson.

Forty minutes later we pulled up at Croyden Aerodrome and everything was transferred to the airport ticket counter. The 24 passenger H.P. 42 biplane crouched outside the ticket shack like some great prehistoric bird, sitting on its tail, its two sets of outstretched wings having a span far greater than the entire length of the plane. This was only a few years after Lindbergh's flight, and the H.P. 42 appeared truly monstrous. We entered through a side door, climbing uphill past the kitchen. The chef was cooking, standing behind great steaming pots, much as in a restaurant, wearing a white chef's hat and a white smock.

We moved into the forward ten passenger first class cabin and sat in large, low, wicker easy chairs with chintz-covered cushions. The floor had a shag rug; long vases containing coral-colored gladioli were attached to the wall. In the center of the cabin was a large, oval, wicker dining table.

Captain Alfred Instone greeted us. As head of Imperial Airways, and a member of the Instone family that owned the airline, as well as a shipping line and coal mines, he was an internationally known pilot and one of the pioneers of aviation. Although our party was only travelling as far as Paris, he was to command the *Hannibal* on the first leg of its marathon flight eastward with an ultimate destination of Australia.

Other crew members entered after all of the passengers were seated. Hors d'oeuvres were passed around during the half hour wait that ensued while the plane was made ready and the baggage was loaded.

By the time the *Hannibal* started to taxi onto the runway and lumber into the air, an hour had passed. For another half hour we circled above the field, gaining altitude, which was why it was often said that the *Hannibal* had its own "built-in headwind." As the sun began to set, we headed off toward the Channel, cruising at a leisurely 60 miles per hour.

It was time for dinner. Our seats were moved up to the table and secured in holes in the floor of the cabin. The door of the cabin then flew open and Captain Instone strode to the dining table, resplendent in a smoking jacket, as the first course was being prepared.

Chrome collars were placed in front of each diner and wide soup plates served and clamped in place. I had seen this done once before, on the French liner *Lafayette*, when we encountered a storm in the North Atlantic. The vibration of the plane created waves in the soup, "whitecaps," resembling those on the English Channel below.

Captain Instone served the Champagne himself, but it was necessary for us to hold onto the glasses to keep them from vibrating across the table. In this fashion, we struggled through a six-course meal, a heroic performance on the part of the chef, the waiters, and the dinner guests, alike. Strict British propriety was observed at all times and table manners carefully monitored. Polite conversation concealed everyone's nervousness that in the midst of all this noisy vibration we were on some absurd, aerial, wicker *Titanic*.

Night fell. We parted the window curtains and it appeared that the wings of the *Hannibal* were on fire as great flames trailed above and below the windows. This was merely fuel exhaust from the engines.

Four hours had passed. We could now look down on twinkling lights along the coast of Normandy. Demitasse cups were collected and Captain Instone asked Fredic and me if we would like to visit the cockpit. As we worked our way forward we heard the radio operator sending and receiving Morse code. He had been in touch with London, then coast stations and channel transmitters, then French coastal stations and, and finally our destination, Le Bourget Field near Paris.

After a description of every instrument, we were allowed to remain in the cockpit and watch the approach to Paris from the pilot's window. For most everyone onboard, this was our first flight, and it was a thrilling sensation to see the lights of Paris lain out like sparkling jewels on a black velvet tray. In one final display of thoughtfulness, Captain Instone flew us around Paris, first in one direction and then in the other, so that the passengers on both sides of the plane could see the city and pick out the Eiffel Tower bathed in lights.

We approached the runway of Le Bourget, outlined by flickering lights. It took another half hour to get down to the level of the field and touch down, after several bounces, where, nine years before, Lindbergh had landed to the acclaim of 200,000 spectators.

After dropping us off, taking on a new crew, picking up new passengers, and refueling, the *Hannibal* departed for Italy. Sometime afterwards, the plane was lost, in Egypt, along the Nile, on its circuitous trip to Australia. The Hannibal was never seen again.

CHAPTER 9

The Teacher of the Year, 1936

MRS. IRENE GUINEY scared the hell out of all the boys in the sixth grade of Riverdale Country School in New York. She was not to be trifled with and she didn't suffer fools, nor did she ever entertain excuses. She treated bright and dull students with the same swift justice. There had always been ways to fool the other teachers but the buck stopped here.

As I moved up from the fifth grade in 1936, gossip and lurid tales of her antics and strict treatment struck terror in even the most courageous among us. When confronting her for the first time, she was a simply dressed woman of forty-something with graying hair done up in a bun on the back of her head. Her appearance was severe and enhanced by the fact she wore no makeup, accessories, or ornaments, and her sleeves were always rolled up as though she were ready to give a thrashing.

At age 10, I had achieved the reputation of "late bloomer." As a matter of fact, I didn't even have the multiplication tables completely memorized and I didn't know how to study. Now I was expected to contend with this shark of a math teacher and I knew I was in big trouble.

Bobby Kennedy, who sat to my right, was also behind the rest of the class and we both anticipated some rough times ahead. Mrs. Guiney had taught my older brother, Rob, and Bobby's older brother, Jack, but each of our two elders had been better prepared for Mrs. Guiney's lessons and for school in general.

The first day of class in late September, Mrs. Guiney introduced herself by turning her back on a class of 12 awestruck boys and writing in large letters, on the blackboard, in perfect penmanship script: "Mrs. Irene Guiney." For some reason, this seemed like a pronouncement of death. The name hovered up there like the name on a gravestone for the rest of the school year, as though it were the Ozymandias of ancient poetic doom.

Then in a voice that sounded like the Wicked Witch of the North she proclaimed, "I am to be addressed as Mrs. Guiney." The other male teachers, known as "Masters," were addressed as "Sir," but she said she would not tolerate the words "Mistress" or "Madam."

She handed out a basic quiz on mathematics, which we were given a half-hour to complete. I got about half right and Bobby said he had done the same. The rest of the class said the quiz was easy and that they had expected something more challenging. As class ended, Mrs. Guiney handed out workbooks and we were given our first homework assignments.

Actually doing homework had never been my finest hour, or quarter-hour, as the case may be, since I had no attention span. This was due to the fact that there was always so much going on in my home that was far more interesting than a mathematics workbook. There were parties, business and political meetings, and lengthy family dinner discussions. I'm sure Bobby Kennedy had the same situation in his home.

Ultimately, I had to show my poor neglected workbook to Mrs. Guiney and a sad thing it was. I was behind the rest of the class, except for Bobby, who had also done some of the work, but not always correctly.

One day while the "good" boys worked, I was called forward to present my daily problem solutions and my workbook. Because I knew that Mrs. Guiney never complimented anyone, especially those gifted boys who were the bright stars in a constellation of mostly extraordinary students, I was unsure what she would do with a dullard like me.

In muted tones, she showed me the error of my ways. Instead of berating me and sending me to the corner of the room in a figurative dunce cap, as I'd expected, Mrs. Guiney found a few problems I had solved correctly, praised me, and told me I had real ability as a mathematician. I, of course, didn't believe it, but then she kissed me on the cheek! I observed the same thing when Bobby brought up his work and we were both aware that the rest of the class received no such grand treatment, but rather harsh comments about not "challenging" themselves.

Inevitably, report cards arrived at home and my mother called me into her study. "We must go over your report card, which just came in the mail."

Woe is me, I thought. This is not something I want to face right now.

Mother insisted and she read to me the report from Mrs. Guiney: "Richard has a real knack for mathematics. He has had some difficulty with completing his homework, but I am convinced that he has the potential to be one of our best students. I look forward to great things from him."

I was hooked and I was revered at home as a future genius. My father, who had been number one in his college class at Columbia, began to discuss serious scientific matters with me. School started to interest me and soon I pulled myself up to the level of the other students, even in Mrs. Guiney's class.

It was all due to that kiss!

When Jack Kennedy was elected President of the United States and Bobby Kennedy was appointed Attorney General, a proclamation came forth: "Mrs. Irene Guiney is herewith declared Teacher of the Year."

CHAPTER **10**

Anastasia, Princess of All the Russians, 1937

THE IMPERIAL PRINCESS, Anastasia, is alive and well, and living in Germany. This news entered our home one day in 1937 despite the fact that everyone in the world knew that she had been shot and killed with her parents, the Tsar and Tsarina, and all their children, in the basement of a house in Yekaterinburg at two o'clock in the morning of 17 July, 1918. Also murdered with the family was Dr. Eugene Botkin, head of the famous Botkin Institute, and family doctor to the Tsar's family. The Bolsheviks authorized these killings to end any thought by some of the simple peasants of Russia that their beloved Romanoffs might regain the power of ancient dynasty.

The doorbell to 1125 Park Avenue buzzed and I opened the door. I was 11-years old and served as assistant door opener when the servants weren't around. The invited guest was Gleb Botkin, son of Dr. Eugene Botkin. He had an appointment to show the pre-publication manuscript of his book *Anastasia* to my father who was a close friend of Max Shuster, founder of the publishing house Simon & Shuster.

Botkin's book was an account of how Anastasia was left half-dead in the basement in Yekaterinburg, and how she was kept alive and escaped, and later tried to drown herself. By 1937, she was ready and able to assumer her rightful place in the hierarchy of deposed royalty. Also, there was the matter of money and jewels owned by the Romanoffs that was being held for safekeeping in the Bank of England.

My father had been in Russia representing some American banks and newspapers at the time of the Russian Revolution. He was present at a number of historic events and was acquainted with leaders, particularly pro-American Alexander Kerensky, who took power after the revolution. A few months earlier my father had taken me to Kerensky's apartment in Philadelphia to see him. Botkin needed my father's endorsement on the manuscript to aid in authenticating various facts.

To look at him Gleb Botkin was a handsome, slim man. He wore a gray suit with black buttons, strictly Saville Row, the best English cut, with sloping shoulders, and a flap back. He was impressive and had grown up with the royal family as son of the ever-present Dr. Botkin. As a carefree boy and almost a member of the royal family, he had formed a particular friendship with Anastasia because she was his age.

He told us stories of life in the Winter Palace in Saint Petersburg, and summers spent at various other palaces, or on the royal yacht. My father nodded with recognition and smiled when he recalled some of the sunny days early in the Great War when things were going well. Life had been animated at the palace, and young princesses and their friends enjoyed a life unequaled by any other fortunate aristocracies. My father, then 25, enjoyed the moment, too, and made a small fortune in various foreign monies.

The account of young Gleb and the beautiful Princess plowed on. I was mesmerized by his description of her, this tragic Anastasia. What a wonderful, sweet, playful enchantress she was, I thought, and I longed to meet her.

She was Sleeping Beauty, Rapunzel, Cinderella, and Alice in Wonderland all rolled together with all the other stories of great beauties and wronged princesses, lost and then found, with which I was familiar. How wonderful she seemed but what she had been through was astonishing. Shot and left for dead, and nearly drowned, she was now revived and roaming Europe in rags, recalling the halcyon days of one of the greatest empires of all time. With Botkin's help, and my fervent support, she would be restored to her position as head of the

Romanoffs, no longer a pretender to the throne but rightful heir. What a wonderful movie this would make! When would we meet?

It was evening. The Haig & Haig Pinch bottle of Scotch was nearly empty. I had been given a tentative half shot glass to show me respect but it was time for Gleb Botkin to make his courteous withdrawal, which he did with old world charm, gently clicking his heels.

After he left, my father and I sat across from each other. Not a word passed between us for what seemed an age.

I finally asked, "Dad, what do you think of Gleb Botkin's story?"

My father smiled and turned to me. "Not a word of truth," he said and I saw in his face the look of a man who has seen through the veils of many a good story.

CHAPTER 11

That Last Golden Summer in Austria, 1937

IN JUNE 1946 I got leave from the US Military Academy to visit Austria where I'd spent the summer of 1937. From Vienna, I drove to Velden am Wörthersee, a small unspoiled gothic village at the end of a large lake surrounded by storybook trees and fields and dotted with little resort hotels at the edge of the water. A cool mountain wind propelled small sailboats back and forth across the choppy blue lake.

I found the Hotel Excelsior after an hour of searching. There was no sign at the entrance. The neglected property was deserted and in ruins.

I walked in the morning mist down the old path to the hotel and to the water where the wooden speedboat had been anchored. Not much of the gray wood dock was left. There was an almost deliberate dereliction, as though the place had been avoided purposely.

Sitting on the terrace overlooking the water, I remained for nearly two hours looking straight out as the sunshine slowly burst through the mist. The sounds of that summer of 1937 echoed in my mind, the Tyrolean brass umpapa, the waltzes, the songs, the violins, and the twin pianos. I remember the scene of happy couples toasting each other at the elegant candlelit formal dinners, and the genial husband-and-wife, the Hecht-Neustadtls, who owned and ran the hotel with loving smiles and special attention for each and every guest. The Hotel Excelsior, Das Vornehme Haus, meaning top-quality hotel, was the last of the luxurious Jewish-run boutique summer resort hotels catering to a disappearing aristocracy.

That last summer before Hitler invaded Austria in early 1938, hotel life went on as though nothing would ever change. Lovers snuggled on the comfortable terrace; correctly dressed old people walked along the garden paths; children played at the beach sand boxes. Most of the guests were well-dressed French, English, and Americans, along with a few escapees from Nazi Germany and Fascist Italy. In those hot summer days before air conditioning, it was necessary to get out of Paris, London and New York, and into the cooler wooded Austrian mountains.

I was 11 years old and the world seemed to me to have been always this alive and so very perfect. Perhaps it is providence that we know nothing of the future.

My mother organized hiking trips for our little family group, up into the mountains near Velden. The hotel packed wicker hampers of individually wrapped sandwiches and some of the hotel's delicacies, together with half-size bottles of wine and Vichy water, all of it neatly folded inside those traditional checkered red-and-white napkins.

Our family band included my mother and father, who remained at the hotel to read his newly arrived newspapers, my younger brother, Peter, who was four years old, and our beloved governess, Eleanora von Schaumburg. Also with us that summer was my English cousin, Freddy Partridge, a boy my age who joined us from London.

The hotel touring car and chauffeur waited in the early morning mist at the front door of the Hotel Excelsior. The car was a 1926 four-door open Packard with a second windshield in front of the back seat and two little jump seats facing backward. The chauffeur, Louis, was a thin, muscular Frenchman with an outsize handlebar moustache. He wore a lightweight, long, beige "duster" coat and a military-type hat with visor that seemed too small for him, but that he wore at a rakish angle, and he had knit and leather driving gloves to handle the large wooden steering wheel.

We traveled at least twenty minutes through rolling fields of flowers to the foot of a small rocky mountain. Just as sunshine burst through the mist, we set out along a thin footpath, gently circling the mountain. My cousin Freddy and I led the party, pretending to be army scouts, while my mother, Fraulein von Schaumburg, and Peter marched together, followed by the chauffeur carrying the food hampers, tablecloths, and a blanket.

This catered climb into the Austrian Alps lasted no more than an hour when we reached an idyllic spot at the green tree line overlooking a lush valley of flowered meadows scattered with brown and white gentle-faced cows. Above the tree line was the rocky, angry-looking top of the mountain covered with stones and a profusion of small spiny purple-flowered bushes and a summer growth of gray-and-green grasses.

My mother took out her sketching pad and told us she would stay at our luncheon camp to watch little Peter while Louis set up lunch. Then Fraulein explained to Freddy and me that we were to search for the elusive edelweiss, the little white fuzzy flower, a hard-to-find Austrian symbol of good luck and happiness, motivating us with the hint that whoever first found the edelweiss would be lucky and able to share his luck with all.

Fraulein von Schaumburg was an educated, attractive, aristocratic German woman of about 30 years of age. She had come to us two years earlier, as a social secretary to my mother, when her family escaped the Nazis, and later became our governess and teacher. She was kind, enthusiastic, loving, and devoted to my parents, but most of all to Peter and me. She taught us correct German and French, and a proper form of English she had learned at school in England.

On the mountainside, Freddy and I hunted happily until one of us found the beautiful, soft little edelweiss hidden behind a rock surrounded by purple heather flowers. We paraded back in triumph to my mother, brandishing the little white sign of luck and happiness, with Fraulein glowing at us with pride and goodwill.

We devoured our lunch, sitting on the blanket and talking like pilots returned from a victorious mission. This was typical because Freddy and I had often talked about becoming pilots. Freddy was a handsome, blonde boy, with intense blue eyes like his father, Major Frederic Partridge, a British Army cavalry officer. Together, we made model airplanes and discussed eagerly what little we knew about aerodynamics. We bonded that summer as "boy allies" ready to go to war and defend our beloved countries.

My mother reluctantly displayed the many quick sketches she'd made in her spiral-bound pad, each one done in four or five minutes to capture the essence of a scene. Later, oil paintings would be based on these sketches but she had nonetheless captured the afternoon's picnic.

Soon, lunch things were put away and her sketchbook closed. Back to the Excelsior we drove, in the open touring car, a pair of conquering heroes carrying the Holy Grail, our edelweiss, back to a cheering and admiring hotel full of happy guests.

They say a light bulb glows brilliantly just before it burns out. There never was, nor ever will be, again, a time like that summer.

I remember most of all the dinners in the baroque grand dining hall overlooking the entire lake with a view to the snow-capped, reddish mountains in the distance. These were elaborate affairs presided over by the distinguished Herr und Frau Hecht-Neustadtls who introduced, with great flourish, musical performers before each pretentious course.

A pianist would play the Venetian Barcarole by Offenbach as waiters marched out with trays of little dishes on which were a few sardines on toast. Jolly Frau and Herr talked about the food and the music as each course arrived, a new soloist and menu treat mingling the senses. They traveled from table to table, chatting with guests, knowing our names and history, making us feel welcome and at home while the food followed, continuous and generous: heavy soups, followed by many meats with knödel dumplings and cream, which was served everywhere and with everything. A violinist played Fritz Kreisler's Liebeslied, love song, and an aging string quartet played Strauss waltzes as the Sachertorte, a rich chocolate cake with apricot jam that was hidden under a mountain of whipped cream, arrived with fanfare on the trays of assorted waiters dressed in the customary white tie and tails, and wearing white gloves.

Coffee was an extraordinary ritual. A tall thin attractive black man, a Zouave, appeared in native clothes, like an actor in *Ali Baba and the Forty Thieves,* with a headband and shoes that pointed upward at the toes. He pushed around a cart covered with a bright red cloth bearing a curious hourglass shaped percolator with a flame underneath. He made demitasse cups of thick, strong, gritty black coffee. He performed all this with the air of a mysterious Oriental sorcerer.

After dinner there was a profusion of liqueurs and champagne for lovers, all carried on a wheeled cart presided over by Frau and Herr Hecht-Neustadtl. At their command, the sommelier poured out individual choices from the various multi-colored bottles, which is when they warmly explained, *"das ist complimantaire,"* meaning "on the house."

Then Herr Hecht-Neustadtl, holding a smiling Frau Neustadtl around her generous waist, announced to one and all, "Undt now Velez undt Yolanda." Out swept the *veldt bekant,* or "world famous," team of ballroom dancers, he dressed in a black Spanish gaucho costume, and she dressed like Carmen.

They glided around the floor as the band played bullfight music. Later there were tangos, waltzes, and even a polka.

The Zouave returned but this time his red wagon carried cigars and strange Turkish cigarettes, flattened, and packed into their original round canisters. These too were *"complimentaire,"* much to the delight of all.

There was still more dance music, allowing guests to try the fox trot and the more familiar waltzes, the new rumba, and the rage, that year, which was the tango. The Neustadtls continued moving table to table speaking scraps of various languages but usually lapsing back into their heavily Austrian German. When they arrived at our table, Frau hugged Freddy and me so hard we looked at each other helplessly. Herr Neustadtl let us catch our breath and complimented us on the victorious discovery of the edelweiss.

Seven months later, when the Nazis marched into Austria in what was called "The Anschluss," Herr and Frau Hecht-Neustadtl went to their suite in the Hotel and together committed suicide.

The Excelsior's elegant guests, musicians, and staff mostly died in concentration camps or in some terrible part of the war. Freddy and I eventually became pilots.

That was the summer of love and beauty, the summer that dreams are made of.

As I sat on the dock of the ruined Excelsior Hotel in 1946, looking out at the lake, I realized that I had, nine years before, caught an early glimpse of my Heaven.

CHAPTER **12**

Nazis in New York, 1938

THE CRASH OF cymbals and the rat-tat-tat of snare drums preceded the sound of jackboots on the street. A marching band played "Deutschland, Deutschland Uber Alles" and hundreds of uniformed Nazis marched up the street carrying swastika flags amidst cheers of supporters giving the Nazi straight arm salute while shouting "Heil Hitler."

It was October 1938 and I was 12 years old. Franz, the service elevator man at our apartment house at 1125 Park Avenue, told us there was going to be a big parade in Yorkville at east 86th Street, only four blocks away. Given my habit of visiting Yorkville with my younger brother Peter's governess, whom we affectionately addressed as *Fraulein*, or "Miss," I looked forward to a day of excitement in the most thoroughly German neighborhood outside Germany.

Along the strip of Yorkville we frequented on 86th Street, which was called the German Broadway, there were four movie theaters and many German businesses, including bakeries, candy shops, travel agencies, stationary stores, beer halls, restaurants, groceries, nightclubs, dance halls, and delicatessens. They were all German-speaking and the basis of a wonderland experience for a young American boy like me. Because I spoke German I was always able to cut through the mystique of the neighborhood and I felt at home eavesdropping on conversations between trades people and customers. I understood the rhythms of daily life and felt like part of the scene, even though I lived on Park Avenue, the son of a well-to-do banker and his artist wife.

On some afternoon trips Fraulein would lead us to Schaller und Weber Delicatessen and buy bratwurst after getting a free taste on a thin slice of pumpernickel bread. Then we would go to the Kleine Conditorei for some tea and *pfeffernusse* cookies while enjoying afternoon dance music.

On other days we went to Café Hindenburg or Yeager House for a lunch of hot *kartofflesalat,* which was sliced potatoes sautéed with bacon. We might go to Die Lorelei for coffee and music or to Café Geiger for decadent *apfelkuchen,* an apple cake covered with whipped cream. Often we'd bring home a little pig made of marzipan from the Elk candy store, the perfect keepsake of our adventures abroad.

But on October 30th, 1938, we were shocked to see Yorkville transformed for Bundesleiter Fritz Kuhn, "The American Fuhrer," who was in town to review his storm troopers, or Brown Shirts, as they marched up 86th Street to the Garten Theatre. It was a thrilling, terrifying, and unexpected spectacle, very similar to other ominous public demonstrations across Europe, but this was happening in New York, my home.

Kuhn was a former Ford employee and had been appointed to the position of Bundesleiter by Reichschancellor Adolph Hitler at the 1936 Munich Summer Olympics. He was an ardent Nazi sympathizer and, in exchange for his support, his eventual job was to run America after it was conquered by Nazi Germany. Kuhn took evident relish at the prospect and in those days the idea of German control of America wasn't so improbable.

The Great Depression had caused millions of hungry and homeless people to doubt the influence of American-styled democracy and capitalism. As many starved and lost their homes and livelihoods, they developed sympathies with more extreme socio-economic programs like communism and fascism. The Nazi Party rose to power earlier in the 1930s when the same set of circumstances in Germany led directly to Hitler's ascension.

By 1938 Kuhn had a mailing list of 250,000 German-Americans with relatives in Germany. Two years before, in the 1936 presidential election, he'd used his influence on behalf of Alf Landon, but had also been heartily supported himself by William Randolph Hearst, Henry

Ford, and Charles A. Lindbergh, each of whom was an influential, anti-Semitic American.

As the Brown Shirts and Nazi dignitaries poured into the Garten Theatre, Fraulein and I were swept up in the crowd. Instead of trying to push our way out, we decided to stay and to see what was going on, and at the entrance to the theatre I was asked if I was a member of the party.

"*Ya, ich gloube*," I replied. "Yes, I think."

Kuhn's speech was in German, and loud and rambling. He said that there were 450,000 Germans in America, and that this force would prevent the US from joining with European allies to oppose the natural expansion of Germany as in the Great War of 1914-1919. Fritz Kuhn said that George Washington was, "the first American fascist," because he had spoken about America not having foreign entanglements. He referred to Franklin Roosevelt as Rosenfeld, and the New Deal as the "Jew Deal." He also spoke about plans for a great Nazi rally to take place the next year, 1939, in Madison Square Garden where there would be 60-foot high swastikas and 30,000 supporters.

We listened to his speech and left the theater exhausted. Yorkville had devolved into a place we no longer recognized and as we walked home, I saw that Fraulein, normally a woman of rare reserve and control, was in tears and shaking.

CHAPTER **13**

Puppy Love on Park Avenue, 1939

EARLY MORNING IN September is warm with no hint of coming winter. Along tree-lined Park Avenue a horse-drawn milk wagon pulls away, followed by a white-uniformed sanitation worker pushing a wheeled garbage can into which he sweeps clumps of manure.

New York is still a manufacturing town. Thousands of small factories release coal dust from little chimneys, dust that rests like fog up to the seventh floor of apartment houses. And every window of every one of those apartment buildings is shielded by a brown and white striped awning that protects occupants from the bright sun reflecting off glass panels below half-opened windows.

The smell of brewing hops fills the air from the Ruppert brewery. Organ grinders' monkeys hold hats out for pennies. On side streets boys play stickball and an old Neapolitan singer belts-out arias for coins wrapped in paper and thrown out windows by housemaids.

The outbreak of war in Europe is a few days old and of little interest to teenagers waiting for school buses painted in the colors of tony private schools in the city or else country schools, mostly in Riverdale-on-Hudson, an hour away. In front of apartment houses, under long entrance awnings, groups of boys stand talking, dressed in jackets and ties, short pants or knickers, with well polished shoes, and school caps, carrying stacks of books. A few girls, dressed in smart skirts, jumpers, or school uniforms also wait, apart from the boys, for buses to take them to exclusive girls' schools. These girls have an adopted air of snobbery, as if to say that no boy really meets their standard socially, and so the boys are too mystified by the girls to socialize and risk rejection.

As I rush out of the elevator on this first day of school, the bronze and glass doors to 1125 Park Avenue swing open and the uniformed doorman announces that the Riverdale Country School bus has not yet arrived. I am conscious of my grinding shyness and very much aware that I am disheveled. Incompletely dressed with disorganized books and unkempt red hair, I am 13 years old and no match for the wise-cracking older boys, much less the sharp-eyed critical girls.

Gathering myself, I look up the street and catch sight of a living dream, a perfect young girl with small features in a short fluffy white angora sweater and plaid pleated skirt with brown leather saddle shoes. She walks a small white puppy terrier dog on a white leash. I am dazzled. Suddenly all love stories, poems and songs have meaning. She is a white statue made of pure vanilla ice cream, and she has a little vanilla dog, too.

Some moments last a lifetime. We dream the same dream and never wear it out. In my 13 year-old boy's trip to heaven, I remember the song:

"There is a lady sweet and kind,
Was never face so pleased my mind;
I did but see her passing by,
And yet I'll love her till I die."

A month later, in the late afternoon, I see her again from the bus window. She turns the corner off Park Avenue with her dog on a leash and disappears. I experience the same intense feelings and now I look for her every day.

When will I see her next? I wonder, for I am going to love her forever.

Another day I see her coming out of the apartment house next to mine but I walk right by her. I am frozen with fear, embarrassment, and feelings of inadequacy.

How can I talk to her? What should I do? I need some excuse. We need to have something in common. The dog! I think, and realize I'll ask my mother for a puppy. Then I'll break the ice and we'll walk our dogs together and talk.

Mother doesn't think Father will allow a dog in the house. He says animals have germs. He grew up in the post-Louis Pasteur era when people suddenly became aware of organisms invisible to the naked eye. I plead my case regardless. I think my mother secretly wants a dog, too.

Some weeks later I close my eyes and see her in that angora sweater and the plaid skirt. I am home from school having done four turns around the block to no avail. At home there is a golden puppy cocker spaniel sitting in my room. My mother tells me I will have to walk the dog from now on. Great!

The puppy is a big success. Everyone I see falls in love with her. I stop in the street while she is petted and finally my dream girl comes around the corner with her little white terrier.

The dogs meet. My dog is afraid. So am I. The dogs sniff around one another but I can find nothing to say. We part.

A week later, my puppy is sick and throws up yellow bile. She is taken to the vet but never returns. My mother tells me she died of meningitis.

I don't see the little girl anymore. After working up the nerve, I visit the doorman at her apartment house next door and ask about the girl with the little white dog.

"Didn't you know," he says, "she died of meningitis."

CHAPTER **14**

A Bridge Too Far, 1940

MY MOTHER HAD a friend who was an attractive lady recently arrived from Europe. She was 35 with bright young eyes and the puffy pink cheeks of a country girl. My mother said, "she dresses like a gypsy," which, for me, meant she was a gypsy princess.

Her name was Madame Maria Meier-Graefe and she had recently escaped Hitler with her older husband, a world-famous art expert. They had arrived in New York with almost nothing but due to Meier-Graefe's reputation as the biographer of Dostoevsky they enjoyed a good life together. He appraised fine art for the Metropolitan Museum and they were installed in an attractive little two-room apartment in the St. Moritz Hotel, which was near the Plaza Hotel where my family lived. It was an easy walk. My mother appointed herself the couple's guide and social planner, and I quickly fell in love with Mrs. Meier-Graefe.

I was 14 and spring rose up in me, much to my embarrassment, especially in public. I realized it was time to put aside childish things and turn to the business of growing up, which meant courting Mrs. Meier-Graefe.

My logic was as follows: this lovely woman may have been more than twice my age, but she was married to an old man of 48 years. At that advanced age, he was probably no longer capable of whatever it is that married people do. Therefore, she was trapped in a golden cage with Meier-Graefe acting the father to my ladylove. Tolstoy and Dostoevsky spent a lot of time on the same subject and here I was in close contact with Anna Kerenina herself, the poor sad lady, with whom I was ready to learn all of the wonders of sex, especially because she had already kissed me on the cheek.

Yes, a month after I first met her, she had kissed me on the cheek at Café Rumpelmeyers at the St. Moritz where we faced the horses and carriages of Central Park South. I had attached myself to my mother's occasional tea dates with Madame Meier-Graef and I couldn't help but say that she looked lovely. She smiled and drew me close for a moment, and kissed my cheek. This was the most sex I'd ever had, except for when I was asked to dance with a Swedish lady friend of my mother who pushed her hips at me so hard I was almost lifted off the floor.

That kiss at Rumpelmeyer's was proof positive that Madame Meier-Graefe and I were destined to be secret lovers. My fantasies extended all the way to how we would face old Mr. Meier-Graefe with our dilemma. We loved each other, we would tell him, and my age problem would soon be solved as the years moved on and I grew older.

For a few days, the matter of our elopement became an obsession. I went over every moment of our future life together. Even if Meier-Graefe would not give her a divorce, we might have a *ménage a trois*. The three of us could get along, with old Meir-Graefe providing companionship to Madame, and me providing other pleasures when I was not in school.

At one of my mother's Rumpelmeyer's tea dates, I blurted out, "Madame Meier-Graefe, would you like to go for a carriage ride in the Park?"

She looked at me with that soft, sweet, country girl smile. "Yes, I'd be delighted, how nice."

I melted.

"We'll meet here tomorrow at three in the afternoon," she said.

I was elated. She'd actually said "yes," the first of many times she would, I assumed.

Mother was surprised by my suggestion but approved of my initiative. "At last you're starting to show some social graces," she said.

At the appointed time, I showed up at Rumpelmeyer's and engaged a big black horse and open carriage with a kindly old driver in a black top hat holding a whip. Out of the St. Moritz Hotel came Madame Meier-Graefe dressed in a many colored gypsy costume with feathered hat and long white suede gloves up to the elbow, and an oversize black onyx necklace with a matching onyx bracelet that was clasped over the gloves.

What a sight! I thought. My woman!

But behind her crept old man Meier-Graefe. He looked like Count Dracula in his old-world German black great coat with an attached cape quarter length over his shoulders. "How good of you to take us for a carriage ride. Just like in Berlin. How nice," he said in his gruff voice.

So the carriage ride took us through the lush green of Central Park. I sat backwards on the little folding jump seat facing the Meier-Graefes who rode in the wide pillowed back seat together, holding hands and occasionally kissing, and enjoying every minute of the trip I'd arranged for my own initiation with Madame.

Upon our return to the St. Moritz, and after I paid the coachman for his trouble, they each smiled at me and then they passed by, patting me on the head on their way upstairs.

CHAPTER **15**

The President's Wife, 1940

ELEANOR ROOSEVELT HAD come to tea at our apartment at 1125 Park Avenue. My mother was raising money for a charity and Mrs. Roosevelt had been the main attraction but she had also been the first to leave, and in her haste she'd forgotten her fox stole. It was still in my mother's bedroom where the ladies had left their coats when they put on their powder and lipstick.

In 1940, before we entered World War II, it was the style for women to wear fox stoles around their necks in a haphazard way, denoting casual fashion, always the highest kind of vogue. Women were not yet conscious of the animal cruelty involved in wearing furs so fox stoles were all the rage and had become the hallmark of Eleanor Roosevelt who was never without one.

My mother, sensing an opportunity to give me a good experience, handed me the stole and wrote down the Roosevelt address, at Gramercy Square, on a slip of paper and sent me to return it. She also handed me a five-dollar bill, enough for the taxi both ways, with plenty to spare.

I was 14-years old and preparing for boarding school. This was my first important mission in the service of the wife of the President of the United States, and I was determined to get it right.

Mrs. Roosevelt was not only wife to the President, she was a force in her own right, a great leader in civil rights, particularly women's rights, and she took great risks to champion the rights of black people. She wrote her own newspaper column, called "My Day," a daily syndicated feature carried nationally, which recounted her varied experiences. She was ahead of her time and had a large devoted following so she didn't spend a lot of time at the White House but traveled all over the country and to remote parts of the world.

I climbed into the taxi and gave the address to the driver. Travelling down Park Avenue, across a side street to Fifth Avenue, and down to Gramercy Square to meet, "The President's wife," the phrase for how she was addressed since the term "First Lady" hadn't come into use yet. I organized a list of questions to ask her.

What is the President going to do about the war in Europe? How many planes can we build? Can we lend more than destroyers to the British? Is it true that Jews are being put to death all over German occupied countries?

I arrived at the house on Gramercy Square, the house that was given to the Roosevelts by Sara Roosevelt, Franklin's mother who lived next door. This gift had produced unusual domestic strain that Eleanor handled as well as anyone could have, under the circumstances.

I went up the steps to the old carved wood door, carrying the fox stole and rang the buzzer doorbell. A housekeeper answered. I said that I wanted to give her Mrs. Roosevelt's fox stole and held it out.

The housekeeper said, "Wait a moment," and went back in the house. When she came back, she said, "Madame would like you to come in."

Mrs. Roosevelt came out from behind the staircase and spoke to me. "Would you like to have a cup of tea, Richard? And thank you for making the trip down here. I'm sure you had better things to do."

I was surprised to see that she towered over me. In simple, sensible shoes she was still more than six feet tall. She wore a plain wool skirt, a matching wool sweater, and a loose cardigan almost the same earth tone brown. Her stockings were a heavy, light brown material and there was a comb in her piled-up hair.

She led me into the kitchen pantry, which had an old linoleum floor and a small table with a white enameled top and two modest, straight wood chairs. The pantry was small. The cabinets had clear glass doors that shown through with cups, saucers, dishes, and serving plates, and there was a gas stove top and old kettle.

The President's wife filled the kettle with water from the large white enamel sink, carried it to the stove top, turned on the gas, lit it with a match, and placed the kettle on the burner. She set out two cups and saucers, and parceled out some tea into a metal ball with little holes, suspended by a chain.

She sat down across from me at the little table, reached out and took my hand. "Now, tell me about your life."

I answered with family items and school information. As she asked for details, I told her that I had been named co-editor of my prep school newspaper and that I would be the youngest ever to hold that post. I said I was petrified at the thought of conducting my first editorial meeting with much older boys.

"A leader must never show fear, not for an instant," Eleanor Roosevelt said and brought out some cookies from a pink colored, tin candy box marked "Louis Sherry" and we drank more tea. She said: "Did you know that the name of our family in the 1700s was van Rosenfelt?"

Time passed in an unhurried way without interruption. Eventually, it was dark outside. The cookies and tea were gone, and it was time for me to excuse myself and leave.

When I got to the street and looked around at the old street lights of Gramercy Square, I suddenly realized I hadn't asked the President's wife a single question.

CHAPTER 16

15 Going on 17, 1941

AGE 15 IS, for a boy, the "no man's land" between childhood and manhood. It's a time when a boy is no longer an innocent kid but not yet able to measure up to adulthood responsibilities. I tried to solve the conundrum by claiming to be 17. This gross statistical lie had embarrassing consequences.

In 1941 my allowance was 25 cents a week. This was a time when small candy bars cost one cent, and double feature movies were 10 cents for those 15 and under. It was hardly enough to finance a life of wine, women, and song, but it was enough to go somewhere on the five cent city bus and subway systems, including free transfers. Or a person could take the 5th Avenue Coach bus system for 10 cents a ride and have an upper deck seat on elephant high wicker seats with a commanding view of everything. And if a person wanted a touch of luxury, taxis started at five cents a quarter mile and moved up rapidly from there.

You could do a lot with a quarter, but there were limits.

One afternoon on the school bus I heard about a party that was to take place on Friday evening at a penthouse at 1160 Park Avenue at 92nd Street. Such a party was more or less an open house to our crowd from the upper East Side who went to the prep schools and boarding schools in the area. The kids likeliest to attend were mostly 17 years old. There would be no parents or other chaperones in the apartment.

I went to the party with Billy Riesenfeld and Peter Buckley. We arrived at 1160 Park Avenue and were greeted by the "hostess," Elsa Golub, an attractive girl with a fetching smile. There was music on records, dancing, punch, Coca-Cola, sandwiches, cake, and much gossip and, most notably, girls talking to girls, and boys in groups talking to boys. Everyone seemed at ease, and I was aware of my own shyness and extreme discomfort.

Outside, there was a walkway around the penthouse with red tile under foot, bushes, and park-like benches. Eventually, I left Billy and Peter, and I went outside where I felt more comfortable, and where I didn't have to pretend that I was older and more sophisticated than I was. It was an exquisite night. The lights of New York were twinkling.

There on a bench was an enchanting, lovely, tall blonde girl. She was very thin and especially well dressed. She smiled and said, "Come over and sit here, and talk to me."

Her freckles and long blond hair made me think of the words of a current love song, "Polka Dots and Moonbeams." After being so awkward trying to move around inside the apartment, this was such a relief. I was thrilled, and I sat down next the girl on the bench.

"I'm so tired of dancing with all those little boys," she said.

"I suppose I'm one of those 'little boys.'"

"No you're not," she said, "as long as you don't ask me to dance."

That seemed most agreeable, for I was a poor dancer just realizing how glorious it is to enjoy a little warmth from a stranger.

"My name is Betty," she said. "What's yours?"

I answered the question and we began to talk about the party, all the guests, and about ourselves. For her, I suppose, this was a chance to get away from the party; for me, it was a chance to get into the party on the coattails of a sophisticated, kindly, older girl.

The evening grew late and she had no escort. "May I take you home?" I asked.

"Really?" she answered so we went downstairs together.

The doorman hailed a cab and we both filed in. I had a little over a dollar in my pocket and I knew that was just enough to go anywhere in the immediate neighborhood, although I'd have to walk back home when my first great date with this gorgeous woman was over.

Betty told the cab driver, "Go to 86th Street between Columbus and Amsterdam Avenues."

Wow, I thought. This was on the other side of Central Park. The trip was going to cost me over a dollar! But it was too late. I'd have to brass it out.

We rode through Central Park, over to 86th Street, and west to her apartment house. I took her to the door of the building and said good-night. Betty was sweet and thanked me, and gave me a little peck on the cheek. I turned red.

When I returned to the cab on West 86th Street, I gave the driver all my money and it was just enough to cover the amount on the meter without a tip. He made a nasty gesture and drove away.

That night and into the morning I walked and I walked, from Amsterdam Avenue to Central Park, through the darkness of the park and then to 90th Street, across to 1125 Park Avenue and home. It was already near dawn and I knew that my date, Betty, must be fast asleep.

Later on I learned that Betty Perske was also known as Lauren Bacall.

CHAPTER **17**

Golden Boy, 1941

I FIRST NOTICED him on Sunday afternoon, December 7th, 1941, at the Massachusetts boys' prep school, Philips Academy Andover. The giant old campus oaks had finally given up their leaves and the New England snows were waiting to cover the browning grass.

George H.W. "Poppy" Bush was two years ahead of me, in the class of 1942. He was Head Boy, elected and appointed to speak for all students at school. A golden boy. One in a million. An ideal combination of physical grace and personal integrity.

The boys who hadn't gone to the morning services at Cochran Chapel were leaving the afternoon vespers services when a rumor circulated that the Japanese had bombed our Navy at Pearl Harbor in Hawaii. During supper at the dining hall, called "The Commons," Bush announced to us all that there would be an assembly the next morning.

That evening I listened to the radio late into the night instead of studying for exams. The reports were chaotic and in bits and pieces. In the morning I hastily splashed water on my head to comb my hair and the water froze on my head by the time I reached the crowd of boys pushing to get into the assembly on time.

Seventeen-year-old George H.W. Bush stood on stage and listened to the explanation of what had happened in Hawaii. He had similar qualities to Churchill: kindliness, courage, generosity, and a form of nobility shielded by innocent humility. With Bush as our example, we learned that our generation had a role to play in the World War. That we must be up to the task. The least we could do was measure up to our Head Boy.

At that time I was an excellent photographer. I took pictures for the school magazine, *The Mirror*, and for the yearbook, *The Potpourri*. On several occasions I asked Bush to pose for me as though he were not posing. He caught on right away and made it easy for me, even during a dance when I interrupted him. He was a wonderful subject and a good model. I enjoyed being in his presence, although he kept a part of himself in reserve, possibly for whatever life had in store for him.

A few days after Pearl Harbor was bombed, Germany declared war on the US and Secretary of War Henry Stimson, who was also the Chairman of the Board of Trustees of Andover, came to an assembly presided over by Headmaster Claude M. Fuess and Head Boy Bush. He explained to us the horrors committed by the Japanese and by the Nazis. This had little effect, however, on those boys who had already begun visiting insults on we "chosen few" Jewish boys at Andover. It was already established that some dormitories and fraternity houses were places we were not permitted to enter, and that some tables in the dining hall were "off bounds."

I had come to Andover with two other Jewish boys, Bruce Gelb and Richard Abrons, and all three of us were in our first year. We now confronted a well-established "new boy" system for the treatment of first year students, which included submission to hazing and other customs that had evolved since 1778, when the school was founded. New boys had to wear "prep" hats and perform various humiliating services for upperclassmen.

In early 1942, Bruce Gelb was trapped by several upperclassmen and told to carry an easy chair from one building to another. It was obviously too big and heavy for him, and the boys were yelling anti-Semitic epithets and goading him as he fell down. Suddenly, Head Boy George Bush appeared and told the upperclassmen that he knew who they were, and what they were doing, and that if they ever did anything like that again he would see them out of the school. His word was law and his presence changed the course of several lives.

Many years later Gelb became a controlling stockholder and Vice Chairman of Bristol-Meyers, the pharmaceutical giant. It was Bruce Gelb who started the first organizing committee for George H. W. Bush for President.

CHAPTER **18**

Longchamps, 1941

THERE IS A place my mind returns to time after time. Warm memories of happy childhood, friendship and early love. Unique moments of understanding and the thrill of discovery of life and growth.

I was 15 and I went to a dance at the Delmonico Hotel on Park Avenue, wearing my first Tuxedo and white gloves. The Viola Wolfe dancing school I attended ran the affair; I knew most of the girls and boys and went to the dances to please my mother who told me, "You have to learn to get along with other people."

I spotted an interesting girl who was wearing a long sleek shiny green dress with matching green shoes. Her almost-blond hair came down like a waterfall from the top of her oval head and her eyes seemed green. She was tall, taller than me, and she looked more like a woman than the schoolgirls I knew. She stood alone. The boys were put off by her apparent worldliness, her sophistication. She wore genuine jewels, not overlarge in size, but richer than what the other girls wore. Altogether she looked like a model in *Vogue*.

Everyone was dancing except we two so I came over and introduced myself. We sat and talked. She said her name was Lustig, and that her family owned the Longchamps Restaurants. I said I loved the food but the overwhelming red décor was too much.

She laughed. "You should talk. Look at yourself with your red hair and your red face." Then she explained that the restaurants were designed in red because women looked best in reflected red light.

Longchamps was a glowing flamboyant restaurant in the heart of Manhattan. It was named after the famous racetrack outside Paris on Rue de Tribunes in the Bois de Boulogne. I visited the racetrack for the first time just after the war. I was still in uniform and I was invited to participate in the opening day rituals and rode on a horse drawn carriage, more like a stagecoach, from the Georges Cinq Hotel with the American movie star Franchot Tone. The carriage moved triumphantly around the track accompanied by blasts on long ceremonial trumpets. This was the real Longchamps.

From one bold and gaudy restaurant, there were eventually 12 Longchamps restaurants in New York City, all looking very much alike. Some said it was Art Deco at its worst, and some said at its best. The chain attracted crowds of nouveau riche pseudo gourmets, fashionable Park Avenue divorcees, and overdressed high level crooks.

The restaurants were good show business, too. Festooned with great awnings of gaudy red leather offset by gold leather with scalloped edges like an American Indian's buckskin shirt, there were touches of black and yellow, and so many mirrors that the restaurants seemed to go on forever. The main rooms were two or three stories high with subtle indirect lighting going down to basement dining rooms and up steps to dining balconies with a Hollywood musical look. The chairs were either red or yellow, with matching tablecloths. Red carpets reflected 40-foot high wall paintings of Aztec Indians. Each restaurant sold baskets of delicacies, chocolates, dolls and toys. Longchamps also operated a catering service, bakery, candy factory, and ice cream plant.

The artist Winold Reiss worked with the world's greatest Art Deco expert, architect Ely Jacques Kahn, to design the restaurants. Investment money came from "fixing" the 1919 World Series through the "genius" of Arnold Rothstein, the notorious gambler and gangster who first envisioned the restaurant for the property he owned on 79th Street and Madison Avenue. His sister, Edith, was married to Henry Lustig, a supplier of wholesale produce for hotels and passenger ships who started his career selling fruits and vegetables from a pushcart on the street. Rothstein put Lustig in charge and supplied endless money from his varied rackets.

Later, Rothstein caught Lustig cheating him and forced Lustig to buy him out. Rothstein never spoke to him again. Then Edith, Rothstein's sister, caught her husband, Lustig, cheating on her, too. She committed suicide. That was 1936.

Meanwhile Lustig made a fortune building up Longchamps right through the Great Depression. His triumph was the 1,000 seat Longchamps on three floors of the Empire State Building with dramatic street entrances on all sides of the building. Fifty bartenders worked at a great elevated circular bar in the center of the grand dining hall. There were 120,000 wine bottles in the cellar.

Then Lustig bought the George Vanderbilt estate at Sands Point, Long Island, very much like Gatsby's storied property. He raced horses under the red and gold silks of his Longchamps Stables.

Eventually, the IRS caught him keeping two sets of books to avoid income taxes and the wartime excess profit tax. He was indicted in 1945 and fined $10 million dollars and, in 1947, sentenced to four years in prison. In 1949 he was pardoned. He died in 1958 at his apartment in the fashionable Stanhope Hotel on Fifth Avenue.

Through the years the food and drinks at Longchamps were pronounced as elegant and smart, which summed up the clientele and the atmosphere, too. The prices were high but not prohibitive. The most expensive item on a 1941 dinner menu was an extra-large lobster, called, "A three claw lobster," for $2.75.

There was breakfast before the office, or lunch after a morning at Saks Fifth Avenue, or cocktails on the way home after a "matinee" at the St. Regis. Dinner was dressy and featured lengthy menus created by experienced old-world chefs. Tipping was not allowed. Instead the proprietors added 10% to the bill.

As a child, I was offered a trip to Longchamps as a reward for "being good," which was documented on a white board on which a small gold star was affixed for every day I avoided being caught doing something "bad." My privilege was the opportunity to select Hors d'Oeuvre Variés from a three tiered rolling cart covered with perhaps 100 small rectangular vessels containing Herring in Dill Sauce, Olives, Deviled Eggs, Shrimp, Melon, Oysters, Liver Pate, caviar, and on and on. The items were endless and so was my selection, until the waiter looked me hard in the eye. Then I knew I'd picked more than too many.

A typical dinner selection: Baked Oysters Rockefeller, Cold Vichyssoise, air-delivered Colorado Brook Trout Sauté Amandine with Seedless Grapes, Schnitzel à la Holstein (breaded veal cutlet with a fried egg and capers on top), Braised Red Cabbage, Mashed Potatoes, and, for dessert, Continental Pancake with Swedish Lingonberries Flambés with Jamaica Rhum or with Schwarzwalder Kirshwasser, a Black Forest Cherry Cordial.

One Sunday I was at the 78th Street restaurant for lunch with my brother and parents. We wore blue suits with white pointy handkerchiefs sticking out of the chest pockets. A family marched in, about 10 in all. It was the Kennedys, in town from Riverdale. I recognized Bobby from my class in school.

Years later, when they were newlywed, Jack Kennedy would take Jackie to Longchamps for dinner.

From 1958 until 1965, I had lunch with my business partner twice a week at Longchamps. Our broadcast media company was across the street at 59th and Madison Avenue. Often there was a well-dressed man near the bar at a small table, always alone. The waiters and headwaiter fussed around him. He wore a dark gray suit with big lapels and a white handkerchief in his pocket. He had a calm distinguished air, except for his ties, which were unusually flashy.

After seeing him a dozen times, we said hello and he asked us over to his table. We learned that he was "The Godfather," Frank Costello, the most famous gangster in America, the only major racketeer who had ever rehabilitated himself and who wasn't on some government or mob hit list.

The waiter brought us empty plates that were hot out of the oven and then rolled over a serving trolley with a rotating silver dome. From inside the trolley he carved up slices of roast beef and served us. The waiter warned us to be careful of the hot plates.

Costello roared: "But the Goddam roast beef is cold as Kelsey's nuts."

The day before Truman Capote died in 1984, aged 59, of an overdose of pills, he wrote an unfinished memoir about meeting a lady at the library in the winter of 1942, when he was a young man, and unknown. He offered to find a taxi for her but the city was covered in snow and no cabs were to be had. He walked with her up Madison Avenue and, at reaching Longchamps at 59th Street the lady asked him if he would like to take tea there. He agreed and she ordered tea while he ordered a double Martini.

She laughed. "Are you old enough to drink?" They went on to talk about books and authors, and she asked, "Are there any American writers you care for?"

"I love Willa Cather. *My Antonia*. *Death Comes for the Archbishop*. Have you ever read her two marvelous novellas, *A Lost Lady* and *My Mortal Enemy*?"

"Yes" she replied and thought for a while. "I wrote those books."

Capote was surprised. Here at Longchamps began what he remembered as one of his "first intellectual friendships."

I invited the Lustig girl to go ice-skating with me at "The Gay Blades" on West 52nd at a weekly event run by the dancing school. We skated together while the music played the Skaters Waltz. We had hot chocolate with whipped cream and donuts. I wanted to see her again so I asked for her telephone number and she gave it to me.

Summer came, and I went away, and then I went off to boarding school, and the war came along. I called her a few times when I was on leave from the Air Force but the number didn't answer.

And then one day it was disconnected.

CHAPTER 19

Citizen Welles, 1943

ORSON WELLES IS the greatest theatrical genius our country has produced. He is also one of our biggest cautionary tales about peaking too early. His peculiar genius was in having the will to avoid compromising his ideals; which was also unfortunate, since there is something perverse in the American psyche that rejects those who refuse to compromise.

Welles rose to prominence in a business that measured success in dollars. Everywhere around him merchants made artistic decisions and it became necessary for him to work as writer, director, actor, and even producer, if only to protect his artistic interests. Over time this caused many in the broadcast, theater, and film industries to feel threatened by him, and to work against him. Later in life he would joke: "I started at the top and worked my way down."

At precisely midnight, Welles swept past the doorman and into the Reuben's Restaurant revolving door. He made his almost nightly grand entrance clad in a black slouch hat, a long black overcoat, buttoned to the top, and a heavy black walking stick. Ignoring the hatcheck girl, he moved among the tables, accepting admiring compliments from after-theater diners.

He came and sat next to me in a booth. I was with two attractive girls, Ginny and Natasha, old friends home from college on holiday. They were midnight supper regulars at Reuben's and had known Welles from previous evenings. I was home from military school and I had lied about my age. Truthfully, I didn't exactly lie, but I did let the girls think

I was older. The difference between my 17 and their 20 was like the Grand Canyon so I dressed up and tried to act older. The ruse worked.

Reuben's, which was open 24 hours a day, was popular with the nighttime entertainment crowd and specialized in elegant overstuffed sandwiches. It was the birthplace of the Reuben Sandwich, a concoction of corned beef, Swiss cheese, sauerkraut, and rye bread with Russian dressing. The late-night upper crust regulars preferred something more substantial and sophisticated, like chafing dish Crabs á la Newburgh, rum omelets, duck with red cabbage, apple pancakes, borscht, and spaghetti al dente.

It was in Reuben's that Arnold Rothstein negotiated the 1919 White Sox "fixing" of the World Series. Legend had it that as he sat in a private dining room, he handed over the first $80,000 that caused uncharacteristically bad pitching in the first two games of the World Series; this was followed by additional payoffs and losses, and, finally, terrible scandal.

Reuben's main room was three floors high and dark in the Art Deco spirit of the times. It was walnut paneled with plum red leather seats, a gold leaf ceiling with assorted mounted fish, and pictures of sailboats on the walls.

Welles, sitting next to me in his overcoat, refused the menu, and ordered Turkey Tetrazzini (a baked casserole of chopped turkey, pasta, and creamed parmesan cheese). The two college girls and I ordered Chicken á la King split three ways. We knew that one order of these chafing dishes was enough for three people, but even then Welles had a notorious appetite. Later in life he would joke: "My doctor told me to stop having intimate dinners for four. Unless there are three other people."

Welles liked being with us because the girls were good looking and they never talked theater gossip. He was called "baby face," and it was clear he was more comfortable being with people younger than himself.

By 1943, the 27-year old Welles was already the *enfant terrible* of the theater, radio, and film worlds. His meteoric rise and reputation stemmed from his production, in 1937, of a much-modernized *Julius Caesar* for his stage company, the Mercury Theatre.

Because my mother had long before decided that I should, from an early age, see all "worthwhile" plays on Broadway, I was only 11 years old when I saw Welles' anti-Fascist *Julius Caesar*. Seven years later I would be in the Air Force preparing to fight the new Fascists. As it was, then, in 1937 I clearly remember the Italian Fascist Mussolini uniforms and the stage that held no scenery, just the red brick theater-wall in the background. I later learned that it was Welles's intention to suggest that Caesar *was* Mussolini, who, in 1937, cast his lot with Hitler after having extended his new Roman Empire with the subjugation of Ethiopia. The play was, in 1937, a controversial risk and equally a triumphant success. Theatergoers approved of the idea that there might be just one way to remove a dictator: assassination.

In 1938 Welles astounded the radio public with his adaptation of H. G. Wells' *The War of the Worlds*. This was the dramatized radio report of an invasion of Earth by men from Mars. There had been a disclaimer at the outset, but few listeners heard it. As the dramatized "news" broadcast progressed, pretending to interrupt another program with updates, hundreds of thousands tuned in, horrified by growing reports of mayhem and despair.

The news of his theatrical and radio successes reached Hollywood. By the early '40s RKO Pictures, after some hesitation, backed the production of *Citizen Kane*. Howard Koch helped Welles develop the idea, just as he had done with the radio script for *The War of the Worlds*. Eventually, *Citizen Kane* would take on a life of its own, without Koch, whose fortunes nevertheless burned bright for a time in Hollywood.

I first met Koch in 1941 on the set of *Casablanca*, for which he would win a screenwriting Oscar. I was with my father, who was financing the purchase of the radio station, KFWB, and we were staying in Malibu at Harry Warner's house on the beach. It was Harry Warner that introduced us to Koch.

I had endeared myself to Harry and Jack Warner, the two most active of the four "Warner Bros.," by making regular delicatessen shipments to them from New York to Los Angeles. They notified me when they were going to have a party and I went over to Barney Greengrass, "The Sturgeon King," proprietor of a delicatessen and fish shop on the upper West Side of Manhattan. I bought whitefish, sturgeon, and smoked salmon, and carried the sealed package to American Airlines on 42nd Street. From there the fish went on a plane to LA, and by messenger to Warner Bros.

When I met Howard Koch, I was almost 16 in 1941. He was kind to me and made an impression, but his employers wished to express more substantial gratitude for my fish shipments. Because of my clear interest in movies and some stories I'd written, Harry Warner obtained for me an offer from the famous Warner Bros. screenwriter and producer, Mark Hellinger, to be his assistant. Harry said that I could stay with him and go to Hollywood High School, which had provisions for those in the movie studios. To my disappointment, my mother said "absolutely not!"

Over ensuing years I came of age, entered the Army, and kept tabs on Koch. By 1951 he was on the Hollywood blacklist, a victim of an ugly period in American history when fear of Communist expansion became the excuse for exaggerated charges and for personal demagoguery on the part of political opportunists like Congressmen Parnell Thomas and Richard Nixon, and Senator Joe McCarthy. Paranoia reached the point where Americans were ready to accept any restriction or even sacrifice of freedom to oppose those they believed wanted to enslave America.

In later years I also served with Koch on the Board of Directors of Superscope, the electronics company that built Sony. From him I learned that, in 1943, when the US was allied with Russia during World War II, President Roosevelt asked Warner Bros. to make a movie in support of our new allies, the Soviet Union. Jack Warner gave the screenwriting job to newly Academy Award-minted Koch. The resulting movie, made from the book, *Mission to Moscow*, written by Ambassador Joseph Davies, was sympathetic to Russia but misleading historically. After World War II ended, when the national mood towards the Soviet Union shifted, Jack Warner fired Koch, who was falsely blacklisted as a Communist by Congress.

In similar fashion *Citizen Kane* began and ended Welles's career in Hollywood, just as *Casablanca* was an early high point in Koch's career that was never again matched. *Kane* is a brilliant, negative portrayal of William Randolph Hearst, the dictatorial publisher, and his mistress,

Marion Davies. After learning of the movie's existence, Hearst was outraged and devoted his newspapers, all over the country, to destroying Welles. He even allied with J. Edgar Hoover, corrupt head of the FBI, and together they hounded Welles out of the country with threats and personal attacks.

All of this unpleasantness was in the future while we waited for our supper to arrive at Reuben's. I told Welles that I had recently met Sinclair Lewis and his wife, Dorothy Thompson, the columnist, and that they had named their first son Wells Lewis, after H. G. Wells, source for Orson Welles's breakthrough radio fantasy, "The War of the Worlds." This boy, Wells Lewis, was in the Army, and a year later would be killed in action, but it was through his younger brother, Michael, that I met Sinclair Lewis when he came to The Riverdale Country School where I'd been a student.

Orson Welles said that in 1939 he had produced radio shows of Sinclair Lewis's *Arrowsmith* and *Dodsworth* for "The Campbell (Soup) Playhouse" on the CBS Radio Network. He said that Howard Koch was able to write award winning radio scripts that shrank the books into a half hour each, normally an impossible job.

He also mentioned that in 1926 Sinclair Lewis had refused to accept the Pulitzer Prize for Literature for *Arrowsmith*, but that he had accepted the Nobel Prize in 1930. Sinclair Lewis was the first American to receive the Nobel Prize in literature. Orson Welles said that Lewis's refusal letter to the Pulitzer Committee was his best piece of literature. Here is an excerpt:

> "All prizes, like all titles, are dangerous. The seekers for prizes tend to labor not for inherent excellence but for alien rewards: they tend to write this, or timorously to avoid writing that, in order to tickle the prejudices of a haphazard committee. And the Pulitzer Prize for novels is peculiarly objectionable because the terms of it have been constantly and grievously misrepresented.
>
> Those terms are that the prize shall be given, "for the American novel published during the year which shall best present the

> wholesome atmosphere of American life, and the highest standard of American manners and manhood." This phrase, if it means anything whatever, would appear to mean that the appraisal of the novels shall be made not according to their actual literary merit but in obedience to whatever code of Good Form may chance to be popular at the moment."

The Turkey Tetrazzini arrived and was served to Welles from a huge chafing dish with a little flaming Sterno can under it. After it was served, the remaining three quarters was left on a side table with the candle burning. The chicken á la King was divided onto three plates, served to my two 20-year-old girlfriends, and to me, and then removed to the kitchen.

I asked Welles why he carried a cane, when he obviously didn't need one.

"It makes me look older," he said.

With the passage of years I've come to believe we Americans should study our relationship with culture. It is not just entertainment; it is a school that the public often willingly attends, a stage for learning about good and evil where perception is everything. Welles may have carried a cane to appear older, but it was just one of many ways he played with us to help his audience better understand the world in which we live.

With this new century there is little to assist our few creative geniuses, like Welles. There is no support system for our artists who face a hostile world, and often sacrifice any hope for normal subsistence. The sad fact is that we often abandon promising artists just at the point when their expression begins to make us see things differently. In Welles own words:

> "I have wasted the greater part of my life looking for money and trying to get along, trying to make my work from this terribly expensive paint box, which is a movie. And I've spent too much energy on things that have nothing to do with making a movie. It's about two percent moviemaking and ninety-eight percent hustling. It's no way to spend a life."

CHAPTER **20**

Poor Little Rich Girl, 1943

THIS IS A true *noir* story involving perversion, sex, murder, and mayhem. It happened in 1943 among the exclusive social set of New York's Upper East Side.

America had just gotten into World War II, and men of military age had volunteered or been drafted into the hastily organized army. Some women were singing the popular song "They're Either Too Young or Too Old."

"They're either too young, or too old
They're either too gray or too grassy green
The pickings are poor and the crop is lean
What's good is in the army
What's left will never harm me
I've looked the field over and lo and behold
They're either too young or too old"
Arthur Schwartz and Frank Loesser

I was 17 and she was 21, one of many egocentric, romantic, but pathetic, poor little rich girls who populated what was then known as "the silk stocking district" of New York. The world had no pity for them because they inherited family fortunes. These girls attract their opposites: penniless, seductive, flawed, handsome, and worthless men.

I was with her three unforgettable times, but I could tell from the first that she was troubled. The sadness was at the sides of her mouth, which tended downward just a little. She had a way of talking and looking right through you. She held my hand as though she were drowning, holding on for dear life. She was beautiful, too, in spite of her eyes, which were misty, and she talked in a subdued tone, a careless whisper. It was easy to see she was looking for help. But she wasn't going to get it from me, an inexperienced boy still in boarding school.

Her name was Patricia Burton. Her father and mother had divorced in 1925, and her father had died in 1940, leaving behind a large fortune.

Over summer vacation from prep school I was home alone in our family apartment in The Plaza on 5th Avenue. My older brother was in the Army, and my parents and younger brother had gone up to our country house in the Berkshire Mountains.

My two friends, Ginny and Natasha, came over in the afternoons to hang out with me in the second floor apartment and watch people go in and out of the hotel in front of the Pulitzer Fountain on Fifth Avenue. It became tiresome.

We decided to meet some of the crowd at Daly's Bar and Grill at 44th Street off Vanderbilt Avenue across from Grand Central Station. This was an informal gathering place for a mixed group of show business hopefuls, rich Park Avenue college girls, and some photographers' models of both sexes. There were rarely more than a dozen at one time.

As we arrived at Daly's there were two large circular booth tables partly filled with people I knew. At one table was a friend, "Gerta," or Gertrude Vanderbilt Whitney Henry. She was my entrée into an adult-seeming "café society," opposed to the original traditional more formal society of her forbears, and she sat with a girl I didn't know. Patricia Burton was her name and she was hauntingly beautiful. Dark, neatly combed hair, parted on the right side, curled on the sides, and cut short at the middle of a soft white neck.

She smiled and looked through me with big, black, mysterious eyes, her dark thin eyebrows lifted just a little. I was bewildered and excited. She had an attractive simple nose and sweet movie star lips, in the deep red in fashion at the time.

Patricia carried with her a little Scotty dog, much in vogue and made famous by President Roosevelt's little Falla. This was a black puppy with a bit of gray on the chin, chest, and paws. The leash and collar were colored in a Scottish tartan. The dog complemented her beauty and, together, they seemed like an exquisite piece of French porcelain.

"Call me 'Pat,'" Patricia said. "I am going to order you a beer"

"Okay," I replied.

"Did you know my father was in the beer business?"

Of course I didn't know. How could I?

"My father's name was Bernheimer, Bernheimer's Beer. They brought their special beer over from Germany in the 1840s. During the Great War in 1918, feeling was running high against German-Americans, so he changed his name to Burton." She said this triumphantly as though she had solved some riddle and was explaining it to a wayward schoolboy. Her eyes suddenly sparkled and her body moved in unison with her words.

Gerta was talking about a party she was having at the Stork Club the next day. She invited us and said to me: "You pick up Pat and bring her at 8:30."

I was beside myself! What a break! Dinner at the most popular club on earth, and bringing the most gorgeous, sultry date. Wait 'til the guys at school hear about this!

I appeared the next evening at 8:15 PM with a taxi at a private house, 315 East 51st Street. I congratulated myself for wearing a dinner jacket with my father's silk Sulka black bow tie and his Tiffany studs and cuff links, all misappropriated from his dressing room.

Pat wore a full-length, strapless, royal blue, velvet dress with old lace trim at the top. Her hair was done up tighter than before. She wore a sapphire and silver necklace as part of a set with matching bracelet and hanging pendant earrings. On her feet were sparkling Cinderella shoes.

What a night! The Stork Club was full of celebrities. We had the biggest and best table facing the dance floor. Food was preordered and delicious, the small talk small and plentiful.

We danced to prime café society music of the period: Cuban

rumba, bumpy with small bongo drums and sand-filled shakers. The dance floor was so crowded you couldn't really dance. But I was glad I'd gone to dancing school, just the same, so I could at least make the motions with confidence.

When I took her home, Pat asked me in but I lied to her to save face. The evening had been just about all I could handle. I wasn't prepared to get into a groping match, if that was what was indicated, and I didn't want to insult her by not trying. At least that's how I saw it in retrospect. What I told her is that I had to be up early in the morning, but I did ask her if I could take her to El Morocco the next Thursday. She said, "Yes." Wow!

The next day, I just had to tell someone about my great night so I called my mother. She listened to my recitation and she knew all the people involved.

"Don't you think you're getting in over your head?" She criticized by asking questions. "You'll have plenty of years to go everywhere, but if you do it all now, you'll lose your zest for life. Watch out."

On Thursday, Pat and I went to El Morocco. It was similar to the Stork Club, but with dark blue lighting, blue zebra stripes, white palm trees, and a sneaky atmosphere.

We had dinner and champagne, and danced and said "hello" to almost everyone there, all friends of Pat. When we went back to 315 East 51st Street, I accepted the invitation to come in.

In the living room on the main floor she made a drink for me and put a quiet record on the phonograph. I didn't drink whiskey, but I thought I should act older, so I did now.

Someone knocked at the living room door. A middle-aged woman in a white uniform addressed Pat. "Your child is calling for you, can you come upstairs?"

Oops! I thought. What's going on?

When she returned, she told me she was married, but she hated her husband; he just wanted her money. She said he got her pregnant and she had to marry him because of their son. She said her husband was gay and therefore couldn't get into the army, but had gone back to Canada to join the Canadian air force.

She handed me a Scotch and soda. "That has nothing to do with you. Drink up and let's dance." She put on a Cuban rumba record and gave me a big lipsticky kiss.

I had often imagined myself in this situation. Fantasized it many times. But I was confused. Now, I was no prude, but the whiskey and society rumba; it was happening too fast.

I suddenly imagined Pat as my wife. I could see her and the child and the governess all attending my prep school graduation with my parents. I was fast getting drunk, and sick.

She showed me to the powder room.

After that I excused myself, got down the steps of the house, and hailed a cab.

Four months later, on October 25th 1943, my mother called me at school in Virginia. I had just come in from football practice. She told me she was calling so I wouldn't first hear her terrible news from anyone else.

"Your friend Patricia Burton was murdered yesterday in her home. Probably her husband was responsible; I'll send you the newspaper front page article."

What she left out was, "I told you so."

When I received the newspaper article in the mail, there was a letter from my mother. She explained that she had known Pat's father, William Burton, and his ex-wife years before. He was bi-sexual and had devoted his life and money to dozens of young men and women, here and in cities in Europe.

One of the young men was Wayne Lonergan, whom Mr. Burton met at the New York World's Fair in 1939. Lonergan was pushing rickshaws between exhibits. They became friendly. Then Lonergan moved in with Burton and his 18-year old daughter, Patricia.

A year later, William Burton died, leaving $17 million dollars (about $80 million in today's money) to Pat. With Burton out of the picture, Lonergan turned to Pat and got her pregnant. She married him for the sake of the child who was born around April 1942.

Lonergan continued his life with other men, so much so, in fact, that in 1943 Pat cut him out of her will. This infuriated him so much that he joined the Canadian Air Force and started a new life while she took up with several men.

On October 23rd 1943, he flew in from Canada for a weekend visit with his son. Pat had been to the Stork Club that night, but didn't return home until eight in the morning. When she returned home they argued but the confrontation ended in sex. When she bit him in a "tender" place he smashed her head in with a candelabra. She died immediately.

He then disappeared, but was caught in Toronto and returned to a sensational trial in New York. He served 22 years in Sing Sing prison and later died in Toronto, in 1986, at the age of 67. A struggling actress had been paying his bills.

CHAPTER **21**

Barracks 15085, 1944

THIS WAS THE year I lived a double life. On the one hand I was the lowest ranking recruit in the US Army, assigned to a barracks of misfits. On the other hand, and simultaneously, I was a night clubbing, theater-going, New Yorker, and a political operative.

It all began in 1943 when I was 17 and volunteered for Army Air Corps pilot training. Everyone I knew wanted to serve, and I had already learned to fly so I had a special skill to offer the military. But my air cadet class was put back a year.

When my class was called to service in 1944, my father awakened me at 6 AM on the appointed morning in his Plaza Hotel apartment. The 2nd floor waiter served me breakfast. At 8 AM a khaki-painted bus left 90 Church Street with every one of its seats filled by a new recruit. I sat with a small kit bag in my lap. In it were underwear, a toothbrush, toothpaste, a razor, and soap.

At 9 AM the bus finished its 70-mile journey and arrived at the gate of Fort Dix, New Jersey, where we recruits spent the day being processed through the reception center. I was handed a file with my name on it, given a physical examination, and delivered a pile of uniforms, and a slip of paper assigning me to "Company C Barracks 15085."

Then we rode the base bus for miles through Fort Dix, the driver calling out barracks numbers and stopping at every corner. When I got off I was bewildered to find that I was the only one assigned to Barracks 15085.

A Sergeant stood at the door and said, "What did you do?"

"Nothing, sir," I said.

"You don't call me sir," he barked so loudly that all the men in the building looked up. "I'm no goddamned officer." He was a typical drill sergeant and looked like Gary Cooper playing Sergeant York, or maybe something like Uncle Sam in the recruitment posters pointing his finger at you, saying 'We want you.'

The sergeant shouted: "If you didn't do anything, why are you here with all the screw-ups, deadbeats, and odd balls?" Again, everyone looked up. I wished he wouldn't yell.

I knew there wasn't a good answer and I also knew when to shut up. So, I stared at his identification badge that read "Sergeant Kowalsky," and I remained silent.

Barracks 15085 was a catch-all holding pit for soldiers with some problem that prevented them from moving along to the next station where they would be trained for their part in the war. The two-floor building contained double-decker beds and no other furniture. Toilet articles and clothes were put in a small trunk issued to each man. At one end of the barracks was a door to the outside, a small private room for the sergeant, steps upstairs, and the latrine with open showers and sinks and toilets. Bare light bulbs hung on wires from the ceiling.

I found a bunk with the mattress rolled back on the upper deck, and I asked the occupant below if it was OK to move in. "You're new, ain't you?" he asked in a deep voice and didn't wait for an answer. "Watch out for that bastard, Captain Slattery. I been here three months and that sonofabitch won't give me a pass." He spoke with an unintended twinkle in his eye. "They call me 'Banker.' I'm old and they don't know what the hell to do with me so they put me in this snake pit leper colony with the worst company commander in the Army." Banker looked a bit like my father. He was a kindly looking, large-faced man in his forties, a few pounds overweight with graying, thinning hair. He told me that Captain Slattery had been made Lt. Colonel at the outbreak of the war because he was old Army, dating back to World War I. But he had been busted down to Captain because he punched a Chaplain in the face.

Banker also explained, in a confidential tone, that he got his nickname because everyone knew he'd worked as a stockbroker on Wall Street for 20 years. When he got tired of the job and the responsibility, he volunteered for the Army. Now that they had him, they couldn't send him to a combat unit because he was "too goddamned old." So, he sat around and couldn't go home on a pass to New York because old Slattery hated him. He had an "S" shaped white meerschaum pipe and a portable wind-up Victrola record player with half a dozen classical music records. Every time he played a record, there was a barracks-wide general disapproval in the form of lengthy "Ughs."

"You can trust Sergeant Kowalsky," he said. "He's old Army, and he really runs Company C 'cause Captain Slattery is too busy screwing the government to pay any attention to the men." He put on a classical record, Mozart's *"Eine Kleine Nachtmusik"* ("A Little Night Music"), waited for the groans to die down, and went on. "See that skinny guy sitting on his bunk playing solitaire on his trunk? He's looking for a game. He's an interesting guy, 'Magic,' but don't play cards with him. He cheats. He never loses. I think he marks the cards with his fingernails. He gets hold of new guys before they catch on. He's got some psycho problem. He's waiting to be discharged. He failed the verbal psychological test, the one where they ask if you want to have sex with your mother. He tried to choke the doctor. Took everyone in the test center to get him off. They wanted to lock him up, but the doctor said his answer was 'predictable,' whatever that means. He has an elaborate plan to destroy Captain Slattery. Nobody really believes him, but I do."

I put on my uniform that was too big for me.

"At the other end of the barracks," Banker continued, "there are twelve recruits from the mountains. They're really good guys. But they can't move out to train in combat units until they pass a test in reading and writing, plus arithmetic. Seems one of them, they call him Stinky, never had a bath in his life. The Captain's gonna have a party for him tomorrow with brown soap and stiff brushes."

At 5 PM Sergeant Kowalsky blew a whistle and we formed up outside. "I know most of you don't know how to march yet," Kowalski said, "but try to look good as we go to the mess hall for grub." We shuffled along with Kowalsky shouting, "Hup, two, three."

The 2,000 man Quonset Hut mess hall was so big we couldn't hear ourselves think. Soldiers doing KP slopped food onto tin trays. The tables were long wood with benches you had to slide onto. We ate meat loaf, mashed potatoes, string beans, two slices white bread, a pat of butter, and apple upside-down cake. Pretty good! I had expected a bowl of gruel.

After the meal we were marched over to the beer garden to have a watered down, five-cent, glass of beer served in a heavy glass mug with a glass handle. I felt proud to be a US soldier having beer, just like in the movies. I was no longer a kid.

Next morning Captain Slattery came over and gave a speech. "Some of you may be thinkin' about gettin' the hell out of here and runnin' home to mommie. Well, I got news for you. No one walks out on me," he shouted. "If you think you'll get me in trouble, you've got another think coming. An hour after you disappear I'll have the whole goddam Army out looking for you on desertion charges. Cowardice in wartime in the face of the enemy is a capital offense. Hanging!"

On the way out, Captain Slattery saw my identification badge and said, "I want to see you in my office right now. Sergeant Kowalsky will show you to my office. I want him to hear what I have to say."

On the way over Kowalsky told me that the Captain had it in for me. He had seen my 201 File, and the sergeant said he'd exploded over what was inside.

I said to Sergeant Kowalsky, "Look, I've only been in this Army less than a day. How could I have done anything?"

"Maybe he doesn't like the way you part your hair"

"Sir, I comb it straight back."

Kowalsky boomed, "Goddammit, I told you about that 'sir' business. Stop it. Someone will hear you."

We entered Captain Slattery's office. The wall was covered with pictures of Franklin Roosevelt, General George Marshall, and other unknown generals and a colonel, the whole chain of command. The captain's hat was upside down on the desk and a file lay directly in front of him, my hated 201. It contained everything the army knew about me: test scores, physical condition, home address, where I went to school, what people think about me, everything.

Slattery was a pear-shaped man with a potbelly, large rear, and small head. He wore steel rimmed glasses. His hair was short in a severe crew cut, almost shaved off around the ears and above where he kept a tuft of graying hair on top. He had an upside down pencil in his hand and punctuated his words by pounding the eraser end onto the desk. He pounded even when not talking, too, as though he needed the eraser to think.

I saluted and stood at attention. Sergeant Slattery stood behind me. Without putting either of us "at ease" Captain Slattery began in a voice that was higher than expected, agitated, and unmilitary. "I been in this man's Army for 27 years. I was in the trenches in 1918 as a private under General 'Black Jack' Pershing, a great West Pointer, in the Battle of Chateau-Thierry. I came up-from-the ranks, and retired as a major before I was called back for this here war. And I never seen, in all those years, anything like you." His diatribe was becoming loud, shrill, squeaky, and emotional.

I was beginning to sweat. I could feel a drop working its way from my hair, down the side of my cheek, and down my neck to my shirt where it joined other drops. What have I done to warrant such a preamble? What's coming next?

"I have never seen a file like this," the captain continued. "What kind of an ass-hole, fancy-pants, tin horn, two-bit little shit do you think you are?"

I knew that was a rhetorical question. I was silent.

"Eh?" the Captain shrieked: "I asked you a question!"

"No excuse, sir," I said.

"Don't give me that shit. I want to know how come you live in a million-dollar hotel on Fifth Avenue in New York, that you went to some pretty boy prep school, that you belonged to some crappy junior ROTC, that you got yourself a pilot's license, and that somehow you wangled yourself a letter of recommendation from some big-ass general in the Pentagon in Washington. I'll bet your Daddy did all that for you." He glared at me and then continued. "I see from your ROTC orders you're a corporal in the reserve. Well, this ain't no shit kickin' reserve. This here's the real thing. You may be waiting for Air Corps pilot training, but I'll delay that as long as I can. In the meantime you're gonna learn what it is to be the lowest Goddam living thing in this outfit. I'll see to that myself. You'll work daytime drilling the new troops on the parade ground, cleaning all the company latrines and all-night KP in the mess hall. Sergeant Kowalski will be on your tail every minute. And I don't allow any of my men to sack out in his bunk during daylight hours. Now, get the hell out of here." I saluted.

On the way back Sergeant Kowalsky was silent until we reached the barracks. "That lousy bastard! He got some nerve. Every sergeant on the post hates his fuckin' guts. I was offered a soft spot in Florida as Sergeant Major at a primary training Air Base with my former CO, but Slattery turned it down three times. That crud said I was 'essential' here. He's cheating the government by pretending to takes groups of soldiers to their new posts around the country when they are assigned. He collects officers travel pay and station allowance for weeks at a time, and the men don't need or get his supervision. As a matter of fact, he doesn't even travel, just stays home in Nutley, New Jersey. No other officer on base does that. The Jewish chaplain brought it up with Slattery once, making a friendly suggestion that he not do it, and Slattery punched him. That's when he got demoted to Captain."

The next month was a test of wills. I threw myself into my work, knowing that I was being challenged in front of all of Fort Dix. I taught marching, cleaned latrines, and taught reading and writing. In the mess hall for overnight KP we washed everything in the kitchen as well as the mess floor and all the tables and benches. Then there was food preparation, baking, and cooking. I suffered from lack of sleep and began losing weight.

One day, Sergeant Kowalsky came to me on the parade ground and said that the sergeants all had decided to do something about me. "The next time Captain Slattery goes on travel duty, we'll give you a pass for the length of his trip, and you can go home. In the meantime you'll spend all-night KP in the Mess Sergeant's office where you can sleep.

After that, night-duty became the highlight of every day. The mess sergeant, Staff Sergeant Valentino Mandrakis, gave me his favorite comic books to read, *Archie*, *Captain America*, *Superman*, and *Bugs Bunny*

(*Bugs Bunny*!), and every night we had a feast in his office. He went into the refrigerated meat storage room and carved out tenderloin "filet mignon" and we dined in splendor, with ice cream and strawberries, washing it all down with ice cold Rupperts Beer. The sergeant showed me framed photos on the wall of the Greek Army marching through the Arc de Triumph in the WWI victory parade in Paris on July 14, 1919 and a photo of Rudolph Valentino, the great silent film star, in his "Sheik" costume. I slept like a baby on the mess sergeant's cot. I had found, at last, a home in the Army.

Sergeant Valentino Mandrakis was born Kourtis Mandrakis in the port of Piraeus, Greece in 1914. In 1918 Greece went to war on the side of the US and Kourtis's father was killed in September at the battle of Doiran in Bulgaria. His mother and the boy left for America in August 1926. The custom then was for the child to be on the mother's passport and he was listed as "11 year old boy."

On their ship the news reached them that Rudolph Valentino had died at the age of 31. Every red-blooded woman in the world was in love with the Sheik and felt personally wounded. The fantasy was so intense that many women had decorated a small nomadic niche in their homes with curtains, pillows and a small bed covered with a traditional handmade Persian rug. What use was ever made of these little shrines we shall never know. At that very point in history, the young Mandrakis entered Ellis Island, having been renamed by his mother, Valentino.

When Captain Slattery took a two-week trip to Fort Lawton in the state of Washington, Sergeant Kowalsky cut me a pass. Off I went to the apartment in The Plaza.

I felt like a hick visiting New York for the first time and I looked terrible. My uniform was, by now, filthy and hung like a sack. While my family was at our house up in the Berkshire Mountains in Massachusetts, I called a friend who was in show business and arranged a big party for the next day in my father's apartment. Then I went directly to the exclusive military clothiers, Luxenberg, famous for doing General MacArthur's uniforms, and had them make me a new private's uniform and hat. I looked almost like a general.

At the party I met a sweet girl from Witchita, Kansas. Marilyn Sable danced at the Copacabana nightclub across the street. She was a dream, so fresh and full of life, and we liked each other instantly.

Most evenings I went alone to a Broadway show, and then we had dinner together after her show at the Copa. During those two weeks I saw "Bloomer Girl," "Follow the Girls," "Mexican Hayride," "Song of Norway," and "On the Town." We dined at Rubens Restaurant, The Savoy-Plaza, and at several of the nightclubs along 52nd Street. I rested during the day and in this way two weeks went by like hours.

At the end of my leave I put away my tailored uniform and hat into my closet at The Plaza, put on my dry cleaned, baggy, Army issue uniform, and took the bus back to Fort Dix. When I arrived in the deep black of night, a thick fog rolled onto the base. The Army post bus picked me up and dropped me off near a barracks building on a corner. I was shocked to find that I was not near my company street, but was instead in a deserted area I didn't recognize. I waited for the next bus for two hours. An hour after that I was delivered to the right street and I got to my bunk in time to hear the loudspeaker blast reveille: "You gotta get up, you gotta get up." Mess Hall breakfast this morning was greeted with almost universal disdain: Toast on which was poured chipped beef in cream sauce and known to every WWII veteran as "shit on a shingle."

I was back in Hades and determined not to be like Orpheus and Heracles. I would not allow Captain Slattery to drive me mad. So, I applied myself to the grind and servitude, at least during the day, while looking for worthwhile distractions.

On a headquarters bulletin board I found out that the Post Adjutant was looking for men who spoke German to guard the German prisoners. I answered the ad, and found myself assigned, in the mornings, to the prisoner compound. I was issued a .45 pistol and holster. I wore it like a Texas Ranger, but I had no idea how it worked or if I could actually shoot anyone or anything with it.

I quickly discovered that the German prisoners at Fort Dix were pleased with their situation. They had full breakfasts, and were allowed to make big sandwiches to put in brown paper bags that they took for lunch while they worked to build more barracks for an ever-increasing stream of prisoners coming in from Europe. Troopships that delivered our men to the life threatening war front returned to peaceful America laden with German prisoners of that same war. This was one of the curiosities of the period. One day the whole thing would have to be reversed. Perhaps the most horrible result was that many of these prisoners of war would later return, after the war, to the Russian Zone of Germany and be sent to Russia, never to be seen again.

By and large the Germans were a dour lot. They were the bottom of the barrel, the last men conscripted before schoolboys and toothless grandfathers took up arms. With rare exception they were unschooled and without any curiosity or interest other than doing as they were told. That made my job easy.

There was one prisoner I recall well. He was well groomed and spoke *hoche deutsch* (cultured German). He had been a waiter in a Berlin beer stub and knew all the answers, a wise guy. He told me in a sly confidential manner: "You and I are not like those others." He indicated his fellow prisoners. "We are educated and should be friends."

This was too much for me, and even though I had promised myself not to reveal my deep hatred of the Nazis, I said quietly, "And what would you have done had I walked into your beer stub in Berlin with a yellow Star of David on my arm? Would you have called me your friend?"

Every night around 10 PM, in the darkness of their barracks, the remains of Hitler's Wermacht sang like Vikings. I listened to them sing "Lili Marlene," the haunting international anthem of all soldiers yearning to go home but knowing that the odds are against them. They sang *"Unter der Laterne, Vor dem grossen Tor,"* or "Underneath the lantern by the barracks gate," the most obsessive and intoxicating, but misunderstood, song of all wars. It is an anti-war poem about a young soldier whose only contact with any woman is a passing word with a streetwalker under a lantern. That's all the love he ever had, or may ever have. And the streetwalker was once in love with a soldier, too, but he was killed, and so she didn't care about anyone. I couldn't get the song out of my head for years.

I also answered a bulletin board ad looking for French speakers and found myself at the Officers Club in afternoons writing menus for dinner. That was great fun! I invented names for dishes, none of which existed in the free world. I honored various cities in the US: Oysters St. Louis, Bananas Flambé Detroit, and Crème de Pois Nouvelle Orleans. Then I honored the Commanding Officer's wife with Fraise de Bois Rosemary, and also our Captain with Salade Nicoise Slattery. That cost me my menu-writing job, although I soon learned that the USO needed someone to make sandwiches and ice cream sodas so I did that instead.

The Captain realized I was out of his clutches. So, he called me into his office with Sergeant Kowalsky. "I hear you've been goofing off again."

Do I say yes sir or no sir? "No, sir." I said.

"Don't contradict me," he shouted.

I should have said yes, sir.

He slammed his hat on the desk. "Damnit, we are getting a new Battalion Commander. He's a snappy West Pointer, and we can't afford to look bad at Saturday inspection. I want you to take charge of all the toilets and make them sparkle. I don't care if they're dirty and rusty. You make them shine. Take all those illiterate bastards and have them scrub the showers and sinks, and don't forget the walls and the floor." He paused to let the orders sink in. "Hell, you're a reserve corporal, aren't you? We're going to be the number one company or I'll know the reason why."

To execute my cleanse of Barracks 15085 I was "excused" from all night KP and, on a Friday night, I was ordered to command the whole barracks and clean the corroding pipes, toilets, and sinks in the latrine. I was issued a black armband with a white letter "C." I wasn't sure what it stood for, but I knew it wasn't Colonel or Captain, probably Corporal or maybe Company "C." Or, possibly it was the only armband they had.

We passed the West Point Battalion Commander's inspection and Captain Slattery took 20 recruits to air crew training in Biloxi, Mississippi. Meanwhile, I went to New York for a 10-day blast of heaven.

This time I hung out at the Stork Club and El Morocco, the two greatest nightclubs of the era. Marilyn met me after her show at the Copacabana and we had dinner at midnight with all the socialites and pub crawlers dressed in white tie and tails. I was in my MacArthur

Luxenberg private's outfit replete with a special Luxenberg Army tie, as worn by General Dwight D. Eisenhower. Marilyn told me she was happy to be on the arm of a private. She also told me she was a Socialist, the kind that advocates government ownership of the means of production. Probably, she was the only Socialist that ever got past owner John Perona's black rope at the entrance to El Morocco because she closely resembled Rita Hayworth, the great movie star. She even posed for Colgate toothpaste advertisements at the Conover Agency. What a beauty!

During those trying first months of my war with the army, she was my only reason for living.

Once when I got to New York five years after the war was ended, my father sent his car and chauffeur to Mitchell Field, in Long Island, to pick me up where I had landed a B-25. Marilyn came along, but, in an exhibition of her finest socialist sympathies, she insisted we both ride in the front with the chauffeur.

She was a good four years older than I, and for a couple years while I was overseas in the Air Force she would have lunch with my mother at The Plaza, and my mother would write me about her. She married a movie actor friend, Dort Clark, and had four lovely girls.

In our New York of 1944, the city sparkled. The showrooms and movie theaters, and thousands of restaurants were filled with musicians. Singers filled every nightclub, big or small. Everyone was aware of the war, and that life was not certain, and that we might even lose, so there was frantic relish in "having a good time." Being fashionable mattered so everyone dressed up; everyone wore a hat and each restaurant and nightclub, Broadway show, and movie-theater had a hatcheck booth. Men not in uniform usually wore white scarves at night because elegance was obligatory.

With the war raging on two fronts many thousands of miles away and across two oceans, the fighting was evident everywhere and nowhere at once. Many men were in uniform; Generals and Privates were treated with the same respect. Those men not in uniform had better walk with a limp, or wear a little gold pin in his lapel, the "ruptured duck," indicating he had already served honorably.

Everything was "for keeps." There was no unemployment and few political arguments. Excess profits taxes covered everyone and corporations. Personal income above $98,000 was taxed at 98%. Life was on hold "for the duration." The heart and soul of every American was with the boys at the front. That we look back on those terrible times with nostalgia points to the pettiness of life without purpose.

Back at Fort Dix, I got two new jobs from the bulletin board: teaching Chinese and teaching English reading and writing. The first job stemmed from the fact that a group at the Air Base was going to the China-Burma-India theater of operations. There was no hope of teaching them spoken Chinese (and I didn't speak Chinese anyway), but the Army had a book of Chinese pictograms, 600 characters that each represented, more or less, a word that corresponded with an English word. So, I taught on a blackboard, keeping one page ahead of the class.

For the other teaching position I taught reading and writing to the illiterate soldiers, including the men of Barracks 15085. I borrowed Mess Sergeant Mandrakis's comic books for the reading classes. At all night KP, I returned the books, dined with Mandrakis, and got a good night's sleep.

One day I was ordered to Captain Slaterry's office with Sergeant Kowalski. "Where the hell have you been? Goddammit, I forgot all about you. You've been goldbricking again! I'm warning you. I'll have you up on charges! Court Marshals are made for artful dodgers like you. I know all about you and Sergeant Mandrakis and the late night dinners, and you sacking out while everyone else works. Didn't you know that in the Army there are no secrets? You are now Barracks 15085 Night Orderly, in charge of all attendance sign in and sign out, and latrines."

Fortunately, the Captain had another 10-day trip to Keesler Air Force Base in Biloxi, Mississippi to accompany 40 recruits to aircrew training. Even though he would actually be in Nutley, N.J., he wouldn't dare show up at Fort Dix and ruin his cover story. So began another great trip to the Big Apple, or so I thought, since I was in for a shocking surprise!

My father had gotten wind of my profligate visits to New York and my reckless parties at the Plaza suite. He knew I was coming to the city, and had arranged for me to work the whole time for the FDR political campaign, traveling up and down New York State for 10 days as a Press Representative with his old friend, Senator Robert F. Wagner. Ten Republicans and 10 Democrats had been chosen to do this work for each Party, but it was to be "confidential" and in civilian clothes.

On my arrival in New York, I was to report immediately to a Major Flynn at Democratic Headquarters and he would cut me "secret orders" to be sent to Fort Dix. I was to tell no one what I was doing or where I was going, no one.

I changed into civilian clothes, or "civvies," at the Plaza, and left immediately for Grand Central station where I joined the Major, Edna Ferber, the great novelist, Frank Sinatra, the new singing sensation, and three chorus girls who were to "open up" each show. I was put in charge of several cases of liquor, and introduced to writers on the staffs of the 7 major newspapers in New York. It was my job to keep the news writers and Sinatra and Ferber happy, and to make all arrangements for their individual comfort. Major Flynn would look after the Senator. It all went as scripted, and I quickly made friends with the news correspondents, young Sinatra, and the three show girls, but not Edna Ferber. She had the idea that I was to be her amanuensis, her slave. At each new hotel in each new city, from Buffalo to Albany and Syracuse, and so on, I was to move furniture in each suite and mix cocktails, and obtain hors d'oeuvres, as needed. At night there were rallies in the largest theaters or auditoriums. The dancing girls "softened up" the audience, and then Sinatra sang one or two of his popular love songs. Edna Ferber, famous author of Pulitzer Prize-winning novel *So Big*, read a passage from *Show Boat*, which had been adapted on Broadway, and then gave a campaign speech.

When I returned to Fort Dix from my 10-days leave, Captain Slattery wanted to see me immediately. His hands were shaking, and my orders were in his hands. "What's this crap about secret orders and civilian clothes? What did you cook up this time? I want the truth!"

I told him I was not able to explain the secret orders.

His face got red, really red, and puffed up. I thought he would explode. He got up and pounded the wall with his fist.

Fortunately for me, everything had changed while I was away. The new West Point Battalion Commander was cleaning house. Captain Slattery was being reassigned and severely sanctioned for his misuse of authority. Sergeant Kowalsky got his transfer to Florida, and Banker was assigned to the Fort Dix Finance Office. Magic was sent to a psychiatric ward at the Fort Dix hospital where it was determined he was as sane as the rest of us.

While cleaning out his desk, Captain Slattery called me into his office and pulled out a letter. "I have held this for a month, but you can have it because I'm leaving. It's your appointment to West Point." He passed me my orders. "When you're a General, are you going to take it out on me?"

I decided not to answer.

CHAPTER **22**

Vous Qui Passez Sans Me Voir (You, Who Walk By Without Seeing Me), 1946

MY HEART GOES back to Bastille Day, July 14, 1946. I was invited to the Paris home of my parents' friends, the late Marquis de Castellane and his wife, French Senator Yvonne Patenôtre. She was giving a Bastille Day party for their daughter, Pauline, who was turning 23, and I was to represent my family.

To me the most beautiful city in the world seemed deserted. Near the Place de la Concorde the cobblestones were dusty outside the American Embassy. There were new brass plaques on the wall that separated the Tuileries Gardens from the Rue de Rivoli. These plaques were dedicated to members of the French underground who fell at the spot on August 26, 1944, the day of Liberation. Beneath them were laid fresh cut daylilies.

As a second year cadet at West Point, I dressed for the party in cadet summer whites with formal high collar. I went by taxi to a deserted unpaved street in a suburban neighborhood. A long high wall stretched as far as I could see and an occasional chestnut tree shaded starlight.

The driver let me off in front of a small gate along the wall. The neighborhood was quiet and dark. Crickets chirped but the silence made me think I had arrived on the wrong night, or maybe on the wrong street.

I found a chain at the gate. When I pulled it a bell rang and an attendant came to let me in. I followed him around some tall bushes and to my amazement I saw a small palace rising from the darkness.

In front of the façade was a fountain framed in light with sparkling water splashing outward from the mouths of stone fish. I saw the building's tall windows glowing with light from crystal chandeliers as I crossed the circular gravel drive around the fountain to climb the steps and enter open double doors.

There was no one to meet me on the checkered marble floor of the entrance hall. I peeked inside the house and saw two curved sweeping stairways leading to a balconied gallery.

A distinguished-looking gentleman in white tie and tails approached. He told me he was the majordomo, the head butler.

I introduced myself, showed him my invitation, and pointed to my watch. "Am I on time?" I asked in French.

He answered me in a stiff English accent: "In France, sir, everyone comes an hour late. Would you kindly wait in the main salon?" He led me through double doors to a surprisingly regal and spacious hall, all in white with gold trim. The furniture was white and gold, too, in the Napoleonic Empire style, and covered in white silk with small gold fleurs-de-lis.

On the wall in this grand salon, opposite the line of crystal chandeliers, was a painting of the great grandfather of the Marquis de Castellane: Marshal Boniface de Castellane, Napoleon's great general. He wore his feathered Marshal's hat, his hand holding his monocle, and on his shoulders were large gold tasseled epaulets.

Minutes later, musicians streamed into the grand salon. They were in full dress as they carried their instruments through the entrance hall and into the ballroom on the other side. The ballroom was the same size as the grand salon. Inside were dozens of tables set for dinner, each one centered with tall white roses in slender vases.

The reception line formed and arriving guests lined up. The majordomo gave my name to the Marquisa, Senator Patenôtre, and I bowed.

Madame Patenôtre smiled at me. She recognized that I was out of my element. "Don't worry," she said. "We're really Americans here."

I was charmed and smiled back at her, remembering that she was a member of the family that owned the *Philadelphia Inquirer*. I also recalled that the late Marquis was the son of Anna Gould whose father was the famous robber baron, Jay Gould, ninth richest American in history.

Madame Patenôtre turned to her side on the reception line and introduced me to Pauline and to her younger 18-year old daughter, Elizabeth, a great beauty. Elizabeth wore a plain, long-pleated velvet gown, no jewelry and her strawberry hair was braided and wrapped around her head. This is truly Juliette, I thought. And I am Romeo.

The guests continued to file in as their names were announced. A string quartet played gently from underneath the two grand staircases. The room filled up with titled ladies and gentlemen, and generals, all wearing elegant formal clothes. Some of the men sported impressive medals and the ladies wore gowns with jewelry in good taste, but the stones were huge. This was the first real Bastille Day since the end of the war.

Then I saw some Americans. Not just anybody, either. The American General Staff. Those famous generals who had fought in Europe and commanded the war in the air, West Point graduates whose names and faces I recognized from newspapers, and from my classes and books on military tactics. They were seated at one table and accompanied by elegant ladies.

I realized that I was most likely the youngest man in the room. I became painfully aware of my simple white uniform amongst the most distinguished and decorated men in Europe. I looked like a hospital orderly or a New York City Sanitation worker.

After drinks we were ushered into the ballroom where all the tables were set with white linen matching the tall white roses. A place card on folded white parchment rested at my seat, my name drawn in florid Savoye handwritten script and preceded by the word "Cadet." To my right the card read "Elisabeth de Castellane." I was the luckiest man in the room!

In front of each place at table was a serving dish, just for display, and a bread plate with a small baguette roll and a round piece of butter, like a coin, with the Castellane family coat of arms pressed onto the butter. There were several wine glasses of various sizes, and the white linen napkins were folded into a crown. Each table of ten had its own waiter and busboy.

The others at our table were young men and women who knew each other. They spoke French faster than I could easily comprehend. We were close to the band, too, and the music was sometimes loud.

A singer came out, Charles Trenet, the composer and songwriter. He was cheered by the guests and sang songs from the 1930s: *"J'attendrai," "La mer,"* and *"Vous Qui Passez Sans Me Voir"* (You Who Walk By Without Seeing Me). Elisabeth loved it, and the others clapped.

The hors d'oeuvre was caviar with a wedge of lemon, chopped onions, and chopped hard-boiled eggs with small triangular pieces of very thin toast. This was followed by a course of poached filet of sole with salsify, a thin white root vegetable popular in French cuisine. The white wine was dry, but tasty. Then we were served the main course: Beef Wellington, a beef filet baked in pastry, served with toasted new potatoes. Red wine was served in large tumblers.

The music, the food, the wine. Beautiful Elisabeth. I was falling in love.

With my right hand under the table, I felt her open hand nearby. Cautiously, I put her hand in mine and looked at her. She faced straight forward as a faint smile appeared on her lips, just for a moment.

Suddenly, one of the generals appeared. "Excuse me," he said. "I am General Gruenther. My friends, the other generals over there, have made a bet. We don't know what your uniform is, or your rank. My bet was that you are a major in some kind of new summer dress uniform."

"No, sir, I am a West Point cadet, a yearling, just finished plebe year."

"What the hell are you doing over here?" He seemed genuinely confused by my presence and then regained himself. "I remember plebe year. What's the definition of leather?"

I stood like a little Sunday school boy doing his catechisms and recited rapidly one of the many things plebes had been memorizing since time immemorial: "Sir, if the fresh skin of an animal, cleaned and divested of all hair, fat, and other extraneous matter, be immersed in a dilute solution of tannic acid, a chemical combination ensues; the gelatinous tissue of the skin is converted into a non-putrescible substance, impervious to and insoluble in water; this, sir, is leather."

"Well," said the General. "Generals Gavin, Clay, and Collins are all West Pointers and they'll all lose money on this bet, and so will I. Anyway, it all goes to Army Relief. I'll be Goddamned, a plebe!" He strode away.

I was now red as a beet, my red hair notwithstanding. I don't think my tablemates followed what was going on or quite understood my intense embarrassment. To be humiliated is one thing. To be degraded in front of the girl you love is crushing.

I could feel her regard for me dwindling. I wanted to leave but on came the next course: cheeses. Each plate came with Chevre, Brie, Roquefort, and Pont Leveque. Rolls and crackers were the accompaniment.

I decided to talk with the girl on my left and use my best French. We engaged in a quiet conversation, discussing the food, and how good the music was.

I put my right hand down under the table, and Elisabeth's was there. Wonderful, I thought. She still loves me.

Then, dessert: chocolate soufflé in individual porcelain ramekins. A sweet dessert wine filled the remaining small glass.

There was dancing and liqueurs afterwards in the grand salon and then everyone was called outside for the fireworks, the Feu d'Artifice, coming from the Eiffel Tower. The sky was filled with exploding color. The band played "*La Marseillaise*" and everyone sang, most with tears in their eyes.

At the end of the evening, Madame Senator Patenôtre and the whole family stood in line at the door as the guests filed out saying, "*bon soir*," and, "thank you."

Making my way through the line, I took Elisabeth's hand and looked at her lovely face. "*Bon soir*."

"*Bon soir*," she said, looking past me coldly into the distance.

CHAPTER **23**

Prince Valiant, 1949

WHEN I WAS a cadet at West Point, I had a roommate named John Sutton, from Kansas, who had the most agreeable personality I have ever known. He was clearly the most popular of all my classmates, and senior year he was made Company Commander and Cadet Captain. He was as handsome as you can imagine, and had an expression on his face that said: "I understand you. What can we accomplish together?"

We both had grown up reading the inspiring comic strip *Prince Valiant*. This was the heroic tale of a fictional Middle Ages boy who exceeded at every skill and, in spite of his noble birth, fought side-by-side with his men, winning with swords, horsemanship, and derring-do.

John lived his life by the precepts of this young hero, making his decisions to equal those he presumed would be made by his idol. This meant he was always looking for a wife to match the beautiful Aleta, pure and noble, who graced Prince Valiant and shared his achievements; someone of unquestioned purity who would live the ideal fantasy with him, and together they would meet the adventures of life.

One evening at a hop (dance) at West Point, Drolette Bradley came into John's life. She was visiting West Point with other young ladies from Marymount College. John was so taken with her demure beauty and her sweet smile that he invited her to the next hop.

For the following few weeks John raved about Drolette and said she was his dream come true. Every day she grew in his imagination. He was "in love," and he told stories about the future, how they would have a family and travel to exotic places as he fulfilled his destiny in the Army.

A couple weeks later I signed onto John's dance card for the next hop. This meant that he would sign my card and exchange the same dance with my guest, Mona Nystrom, a lovely blonde Swedish girl. That's how I met Drolette Bradley from Clark, Missouri.

She was everything John said, and more. A small, slim, dark-haired beauty. She was graceful, and spoke with an enchanting voice. A fitting mate, I thought, for Prince Valiant.

As we danced, I asked her how she acquired the name Drolette.

"In my town almost everybody is named Bradley," she explained. "So they selected unusual first names. Omar Bradley, the five star general, is from Clark."

I would have gone for Drolette, but John had declared her his "OAO," his "one and only." It was not permitted to poach on a roommate's OAO. Not that I could have taken her away from John if I had tried, but she did smile at me in a confidential sort of way.

Mona Nystrom was my guest for the weekend of the hop. She was, to me, a sort of sister. My mother knew her parents in Sweden and sent her up to visit with us on winter sports weekends. She was a champion skier and excellent dancer. We corresponded often.

Here, we come to the turning point in my story.

One day John asked if he could speak with me on a confidential matter.

"Of course," I said. We had sometimes spoken freely.

"Drolette is Catholic," he said.

This didn't concern me at all. As far as I was concerned, one Christian was as good as another.

"But my family wouldn't accept a Catholic." He lapsed into talk about Prince Valiant, who I assume was not Catholic either. Then he said that Aleta, Valiant's wife, had golden blonde hair.

Now it developed that John had already met the Aleta of his dreams. Her name was Dana. A delightful flaxen-haired girl who was the perfect image of a wife for Prince Valiant.

Graduation was coming, along with all the festivities, parades, and the graduation hop. Given his developing love for Dana, John didn't know what to do about Drolette. He was troubled about not hurting her feelings because she was friends with everyone in the company and naturally would expect to be invited.

I volunteered to invite her and her lovely mother who was coming in from Clark, Missouri. My father, who had been widowed two years before, agreed to escort Mrs. Bradley to graduation. And that's how my father and I had two of the best-looking ladies at the West Point Graduation on June 7, 1949.

Eventually, John and Dana were married, and, like Prince Valiant and Aleta, they lived happily ever after.

CHAPTER **24**

Fritz, The Flying Dog, 1949

Part 1

IN 1949 I was an Army officer at The Ground General School at Fort Riley, Kansas. My family and friends were particularly impressed that I rose so quickly in the Army that I was now attending a school for generals. In truth, though, it was really a second boot camp meant to acquaint Army officers with specific Army functions, such as cooking for a 2,000 man mess hall, or keeping track of thousands of blankets.

One day, in the midst of my duties, I saw a "For Sale" ad in the Junction City newspaper. On impulse, I sent in a check and a couple weeks later I received a postcard from the main post office at Fort Riley stating that a parcel had arrived, and that I must pick it up immediately.

The "parcel" was a small box with holes punched in it and a big red arrow pasted on the side with the words: "Livestock, this side up." Inside the box was a tiny animal, a handful, no more, but he was, indeed, a genuine boxer puppy with pointy ears and a small bobtail.

I had always loved boxers; their coat is short and shiny like that of a horse. It's a real man's dog with a tough-looking square head that features a receding nose and alert ears. The breed was developed in Germany where they were called *bullenbeisers*, bull biters, since they had been used in the ancient German version of bull fighting which pitted dogs against bulls. That accounted for the receding nose, which allowed them to breath while their teeth were embedded in bull flesh.

My puppy had a brownish coat with four white paws and a white chest, and I preferred to think that he was descended from a branch of boxers who would rather smell flowers than kill. I named him "Fritz" and registered him with the Westminster Kennel Club as Fritz von Rosenblatt.

Fritz fit easily into the patch pocket of my field jacket. As small as he was, he was not allowed in the Bachelor Officers' Quarters but still went with me to all our training classes until he grew too large for my pocket and too big for me to hide in the BOQ. Then I was obligated to rent a minuscule basement apartment in Junction City and we set up housekeeping together.

Fritz was a good roommate. He always looked me straight in the eye, and with a loving, questioning tilt of the head. He slept at the end of my bed next to my feet, and as he grew bigger, he covered my feet. Some mornings I had trouble getting up and standing because of the weight of his body on my ankles, eventually 50 or 60 pounds.

I tried to teach him to sleep on the floor but at first it didn't take. He would jump on the bed, and then look up at me to see what would happen next. I'd scold him and then he'd go back to his blanket on the floor. Still, I would wake up in the morning with him in bed on top of my feet. He even learned to jump off the bed when he heard me coming back down the hall, but the springs of the bed would still be shaking so I knew that he had been there.

From Fort Riley, I went on to Fort Sill to The Artillery School, then back to my original WWII branch, the Air Force. Pilot training was in San Angelo, Texas, and then Advanced Multi Engine in Enid, Oklahoma.

By that time Fritz was full-grown and the best-looking boxer you've ever seen. As a matter of fact, he won Best Male of Breed in the Dallas Annual Dog Show, an impressive big blue ribbon with a rosette at the top.

The Air Force was more open-minded than the stiff Army had been, and I was allowed to bring Fritz to the flight line where he became squadron pet. When we flew B-25s I'd sneak him on board and that's how his flying career began.

At first, he was confused by the unsteady footing, but he soon learned to enjoy the gentle movement and lay on his blanket next to the engineer, who sat behind the pilots. But he always kept one eye open, just in case.

He tolerated my girlfriends, too, insisting on going on drives with us in my open sage green Oldsmobile. He'd sit up front on the red leather seat and survey the countryside from the right hand window while my girlfriend complained about being pushed into the middle. Any girl who didn't like this arrangement didn't stand a chance.

In 1951 I received orders to go to Wiesbaden, Germany, to Headquarters USAF Europe. I was to take my baggage and the Oldsmobile to the transport ship from Brooklyn Navy Yard to Bremen, Germany. My orders stated "how to take dependents to the ship," together with baggage, household goods, "and pets." I would have my pet inspected and placed in a large crate, and put in the care of a veterinary officer who would, the next day, be on the ship with us.

I said goodbye to Fritz; unfortunately, it would be a month before I saw him again. That night I received urgent orders to go to Mitchell Field in Long Island, NY, and fly directly to Wiesbaden. There had been a crisis with the Russians and I was needed to translate for an Air Force General. It was flattering and exciting; but, though I was trained in Russian, I knew I wasn't qualified for the work. I also knew that in the Air Force you never say you can't do something. Fritz would be sailing without me.

The next day I was in Wiesbaden. The C-54 four-engine transport landed at Rhein-Main Air Force Base at Frankfurt, in the US Zone, Occupied Germany. All passengers and their gear were dumped into the back of a heavy duty Army truck, and we rode on wooden side benches through towns and countryside to picturesque Wiesbaden, untouched by the war which had served to devastate the rest of Germany.

For me, Germany held strange nostalgic value. As we passed through ancient towns, I heard voices speaking German and understood every word. This was the country of my ancestors; my great grandparents sailed to America in 1841, but continued to speak German at home in Virginia. Yet this Germany was also the land that would have happily put me to death had I been living there 6 years before.

As we bounced along over old cobblestone streets I remembered the haunting musical strains of Fritz Kreisler's violin concerto, "Capriccio Viennois." A single violin crying vibrato about the old days, and echoing sadly "look at us now."

I reported to General Crawford and discovered I was to be his aide with the following extensive title; "Administrative Assistant to the Assistant Chief of Staff A-4 for Materiel and Supply US Air Force Europe." There were other titles involving NATO and Allied Air Forces of Northern Europe, and I was given a very small desk outside Gen Dennison's office. His title was Chief of Staff to the Assistant Chief of Staff, etc., and I was the only Lieutenant in the building.

General Dennison asked about my family. I explained that I was unmarried but that I had a dog coming on an Army transport, and that the dog was my "dependent."

"How the f... did that happen?" he asked.

"I don't know," I said, having long before learned that a junior officer does not comment to a senior on the vagaries of military policy, although I just had, so I changed the subject, still another rule breaker. "Sir, I understand I was rushed over here because of an emergency."

"The 'Rooskies' backed down," he said, and that was all I ever heard about "the emergency" that took me to Wiesbaden. Then the general explained that I couldn't keep a dog in the BOQ. "It's against regulations."

I answered sheepishly and proudly, "Sir this dog is a 'dependent.'"

"Jesus Christ, I don't want to hear about that Goddamn dog again; I've got an Air Force to run!"

He suggested I go see Sergeant Major Brodsky who was in charge of all non-military matters for General Updegraff, Base Commander of Wiesbaden. On my way out, Dennison said, "This guy, Brodsky, is the world's greatest scrounger."

A word of explanation concerning this time in the history of the Air Force: This was shortly after World War II and the men I'm writing about were the survivors of the most vicious and deadly war in history that, for them, was fought miles above the earth in mass-produced airplanes, many of which crashed and burned long before they even sighted the enemy.

The chances of an airman staying alive in a bomber from the

beginning of the war to the end were zero. We won the air war because we could manufacture planes and train pilots faster than the enemy.

After the war, Air Force discipline had been relaxed. In a way, my arrival on scene with Fritz, my "dependent," that "Goddamn dog," and Sergeant Major Jake Brodsky, "the world's greatest scrounger," were symptomatic of the time.

I found Sergeant Brodsky in a small, square new red brick building in the center of the walled-in caserne which served as barracks for the Air Force in Wiesbaden. Downstairs was a brightly lit bowling alley and a soda fountain serving hot dogs, hamburgers, coffee, and milkshakes. Airmen were bowling and enjoying snacks at round tables. Attractive young German girls dressed in red and white Tyrolean dirndl dresses set pins at the other end of the alleys and also worked behind the snack counter.

Brodsky was upstairs behind a closed door that had a sign: "Absolutely No Entry... COGEN CLUB." I entered and met the mustachioed, heavyset Brodsky, who was in his underwear in a lavish room furnished like an 18th century Versailles reception hall. At the rear of the room was an open double door to the sergeant's grandiose bedroom furnished in early San Francisco Bordello with a king-size bed covered by a golden quilt with tassels. Behind the bedroom was a large gleaming white tile bathroom. We talked for a long time while he dressed and simultaneously told me the story of the building.

He had somehow mesmerized General Updegraff into allowing him to design and build this bowling alley. He'd convinced the General that the enlisted men needed a recreational building in order to keep them out of the "fleshpots" of lower Wiesbaden, although I later discovered that there were no such fleshpots.

Sergeant Brodsky told me in, strictest confidence, that he had two sets of plans drawn up: one with an upstairs and one without. He'd shown the General the one-story plans, but built the two-story blueprint with a palatial suite for himself upstairs. After some time, word got out, so the Sergeant established the COGEN CLUB: Colonels and Generals, but full "bird" Colonels and Generals only, with one night a week set aside for these officers, of whom there were many, to bowl and go upstairs and do some serious drinking. COGEN CLUB members were served by the best looking bar girls and pin spotters. It was a chance for these distinguished flyers to escape the tedium of married life and the loneliness of high command.

At first Jake Brodsky had treated me like a company spy. As a West Point graduate, I was like the boss's son, and he assumed I was some kind of snot-nosed snitch sent around to get some dirt on him. After telling him about Fritz and some of my observations about my eight years under military rule, he warmed up and we became lifelong friends.

He showed me to an empty room on the main floor of his little kingdom and went off in his jeep to fetch me a mattress for the room. He took along a displaced person, a thin little man in a big gray felt hat whom he called Mr. *Umsunst*, which means, literally, "and so what?" He was Jake's shadow who followed him everywhere.

He told me that the girls would take care of my room and my dog, and with a little sparkle in his eye, he said, "and you, too." I eventually became a champion bowler and one night I won enough money to buy a brand new Cadillac convertible.

Two weeks later I was notified that my "dependents" and my Oldsmobile would arrive at Bremerhaven, up north near Bremen and that I had orders to go get them. I hopped a ride on a C-47 up to Hamburg and rode an Army truck over to Bremerhaven just in time to attend the docking of the transport ship. The Army band was playing and a long red carpet stretched to the gangplank. On shore I stood with all the uniformed American men waiting for their families to come on shore. Cranes lifted cargo from the hold. Wives and children poured out onto the red carpet while the band played "Happy Days Are Here Again" and "The Stars And Stripes Forever."

On the pier I found Fritz in a playpen. He jumped with joy and looked bright and happy. Some of the families came over to tell me he was the most popular pet on the ship. Fritz looked at me and tilted his head, as if to say "where have you been?" I was given a certificate for a room at the Army Hotel and invited to the "Welcome to Germany" gala dinner. With my car on shore, with Fritz at hand, and my trunk in the back, we drove off to the hotel. We were like lovers reunited.

On the way back to Wiesbaden, we took the scenic route with Fritz seated to my right and his head out the open window in the manner dogs love so much, sucking in the air as it compressed against his nose and open mouth. The countryside was dark green with rolling pine trees and occasional quaint old villages and people going about in their customary, timeless, farming pursuits. In the open country there was no sign of the war or of Hitler, or of any resentment towards Americans. Everywhere, girls and children waived and blew kisses to Fritz, for this was a land of universal love of dogs, but especially boxers.

There was a notable absence of men, the inevitable result of recent wars in Spain, North Africa, France, Italy, Russia, and in all the skies and seas of the world. That was the invisible elephant in every room of postwar Germany; it was a country without men.

Fritz and I settled down to our life together in a sort of chicken ranch built on an ancient Anglo Saxon fort now used for housing American airmen in the center of Wiesbaden. All around us were the sounds of bugles announcing reveille, assembly, retreat at the lowering of the flag, and, at last, mercifully, taps and lights out.

One day Jake took Fritz and me in his Jeep to see his friend, Herr Walther Blohm and Blohm's family who lived in a sumptuous estate just outside Wiesbaden. The house was a long country mansion with acres of green golf course type grasses, the sort of place you see on old sepia postcards. There were Herr Blohm, middle aged, young Frau Blohm, and two boys, about six and 10. They were all very correct and genuinely friendly.

Jake said, "Herr Blohm takes care of us very well," and jabbed me in the side with his elbow. "Frau Blohm's family owns some big cafes and restaurants in Wiesbaden. He gets me things the Air Force can't get."

The boys played with Fritz all afternoon while Jake and I talked to the Blohms over tea in the well-furnished living room. It was a nice visit.

Years later I discovered that Herr Blohm was an owner of Blohm & Voss that built German battleships in the two World Wars. He had turned to making machines that made stockings. This was a necessary commodity in Jake Brodsky's trading enterprises, and the reason for making their acquaintance.

A week after our tea, Fritz disappeared from Jake's bowling alley. He was found at the Blohm's house with the boys. They said they loved *"Unser Fritz,"* our Fritz, when I arrived to pick him up.

Each day at the bowling alley at the caserne the clop, clop of marching boots; and the growl of military vehicles filled the air. At night Fritz and I listened to the sounds of bowling pins and the roar of excitement and laughter of young men at play.

This didn't last for long, however. Eventually, Washington decided that the emergency with the Russians wasn't going to recur, and we began closing out the Berlin Airlift. My days of hanging around were over, and I was sent to Rhein Main Air Force Base at nearby Frankfurt-am-Main to fly in an operational unit on a daily basis. I bid goodbye to General Crawford, to Generals Dennison and Updegraff, to Sergeant Major Jake Brodsky, to little Mr. Umsunst, and to a bevy of giggling beauties who were, at the end, in tears at their genuine loss of their *seusse loytnant*, or "sweet lieutenant," and *kleine Fritzy*, their little Fritz.

There was a ceremony in the bowling alley snack room where my favorite bar girl presented Fritz with a giant bone almost the size of a dinosaur's elbow done up in a red bow. Jake gave Fritz an Army K-9 Corps winter raincoat, and Fritz licked his face in return.

And so my little family, Fritz and I, drove off to Frankfurt, in my Oldsmobile with the top down. My Army trunk was in the back seat sticking up, and Fritz assumed his usual position in front riding shotgun.

Frankfurt proved strictly military. I reported in and was given my squadron assignment and a slip for the BOQ, which Fritz and I discovered was a recently constructed single-story rectangular building with faceless Scandinavian furniture. As we approached the desk, the civilian German manager stood up and wagged his index finger while his face grew red, and he boomed out: "Achtung ! Kein Hunde," Watch Out, No Dogs.

Fritz and I retreated to my car and back to the housing administrator. She was a trim Air Force Captain, about 10 years older than I, who had the efficient look of a career schoolmarm or librarian. I told her we had just been thrown out of the BOQ, and that I hadn't even had the opportunity to explain to the manager that this was not some ordinary mutt, but a full-fledged legal "dependent," and also a bachelor, but I'm afraid my sarcasm was lost on the woman, who immediately recited to me, by memory, a specific regulation preventing any "pet" from being housed in any BOQ.

When I explained to her that the government had gone to great expense to bring this boxer from America, because he was my "dependent," we both looked down at the dog. Fritz seemed to know it was his cue to tilt his head.

The Captain said that there was a place to board animals, and pulled out a card printed in German which stated the daily costs involved. This was a game I knew how to play and I replied that since the dog was a dependent, the Air Force would have to pay for housing Fritz. She replied that there is no appropriation for boarding a dog, and around and around we went.

Finally, the lady Captain shouted, "I can't stand the BOQ! I've been living there two years in a single room like a prisoner." Her eyes filled up and she looked at me with a wounded expression.

A little time passed. "Let's get married," she said.

Shocked, I made no reply.

"Oh, I wouldn't make any demands on you; we could divorce any time you say, I'll put it in writing." Now she was crying. "It's just that if we married, we could have a real home, with a maid and a kitchen and bedrooms and baths, and a yard for your dog, all at government expense." The crying resumed. "I'm in charge of housing, and I have this lovely house picked out near here in Zeppelinheim. It belongs to the US and it's ready for a small family."

Here I was, a First Lieutenant, with a superior officer, a Captain, pouring out her heart to me. As a rule I don't lie, except under the most extreme circumstances, and only when it is for the good of others. So I lied: "I am engaged to marry."

She looked straight at me and exhaled with a sigh. "Oh." She pulled herself together, dried up her face with a handkerchief, fished out a small compact and applied powder slowly to her reddened nose. She nodded to me in total defeat and said, "you won't mention this to anyone, will you?"

I agreed with a nod.

"You will have that house!" she said.

So that's how Fritz and I came to have a lovely little house on the outskirts of Frankfurt-am-Maine in Occupied Germany in 1951.

Part 2

The next day Fritz and I rode out to Zeppelinheim in my green Olds convertible with my trunk and some bedding borrowed from the Quartermaster. We found the house on a charming street, tree lined with bright green leaves as big as your hand. In front of each house there was a grass lawn with a white picket fence and gate.

There at the open door, like in a fairy tale, stood our very own storybook maid. She had yellow gold hair braided into twin pigtails and tied with blue bows that matched her blue eyes. Red-topped apple cheeks, no makeup, a candy striped blue and white dress covered with an embroidered white maid's smock, white socks and sneakers. She was leaning against the open door with a simple broom in her hand waiting for our arrival.

I wasn't a religious person, and neither was Fritz, but we had both just fallen into something for which there was no explanation other than divine intervention. A little white lie produced this magic kingdom complete with a candy-striped princess named Gretel, so much like Rapunzel of the long golden hair.

She led us into the fully furnished house. On the reception table in the entrance hallway lay receipts for the house, the furniture, and the maid. Also, there was a commissary card and a formal welcome note from the military housing division signed by the lady Captain.

Gretel took me upstairs into the master bedroom and showed me the master bath. Then we toured the guest rooms and bath; and upstairs on the third floor was the attic. She decided that Fritz would sleep downstairs near her maid's room behind the kitchen.

So began two glowing weeks for Fritz and me. I spent days at the air base bringing my flying skills up to level and evenings were full of joy playing house in Zeppelinheim.

Very early in the mornings: *Fruhstuck*, breakfast, was waiting for me, piping hot, on the dining room table. In a bowl was Muesli, a granola cereal with seeds and bits of dried fruit. *Brötchen*, little hot rolls, lay next to a jar of honey. *Ei auf brot*, egg on German bread with a grilled tomato and *white wurst*, a fat white sausage. The coffee was black and strong.

For Fritz, Gretel made a mush of hamburger meat, egg and Muesli, which he enjoyed immensely. We dined together in lonely splendor like a pasha and his favorite pet.

At 5:30 AM, Fritz and I jumped into our Oldsmobile and said *"auf viedersehen"* to Gretel. She said she would clean the house and get started with dinner. One morning, on the way to the Air Base, it occurred to me that I should ask the lady housing Captain to have dinner with us as a sign of my gratitude. On the other hand, I realized, this was a bad idea since my flimsy engagement story would create some questions about my domestic arrangement with Gretel.

At Rhein-Main Air Base, the 60th Troop Carrier Wing had squadron shacks along concrete pads where our twin engine C-82s were parked. Each shack had an operations room, a bathroom and a general squadron room for the pilots to relax in, and for briefings.

Our squadron handyman groundskeeper was a stateless, displaced person from Yugoslavia whose first name was Hrvoje. No one could pronounce this, so he was called Hugo in honor of his origin, Yugoslavia, which is where he had lost his wife and children in the war. There was something to do with the underground and the resistance but to what, and on which side he was on, I didn't know. But he could no longer go home; he'd lost his papers, and like so many other people in Europe, then, like Jake Brodsky's Mr. Umsunst, he struggled to find work and a place to live.

Hugo had a worn face with tracks of lines crossing each other leaving hundreds of little squares from ear to ear. He wore discarded clothing that made him look like part of our beat-up squadron shack. Hugo immediately fell in love with Fritz, giving him water and putting him gently into his fenced-in garden in front of our shack, where Hugo grew flowers and vegetables.

Three of my West Point classmates were in the squadron. When asked about where I was living, and how I got a house when I wasn't even married, my story about Fritz was hard to accept until I brought in all the official papers.

After two weeks of flying to Oslo, Cairo, Casablanca and Tripoli as co-pilot, I was ready for a check ride with Colonel Gray, our Squadron Commander. The Colonel was a gentle, handsome and popular leader, and was respected for his spotless career and for his genuine care for his men. Nevertheless, these rides were nerve-racking because I was always worried I would do something stupid.

To my surprise, the Colonel said, "I'll fly. I want to talk to you. It's come to my attention that you have a house in Zeppelinheim and that you are a bachelor and that there is a teenage German girl living with you. That does not reflect well on the service."

"Sir," I began, hoping formality would win the day. "This girl is a maid who was assigned to the house by the Air Force Housing Administratress. I am not involved with her in a personal way."

"Okay," he said. "Get rid of her."

The rest of the ride was a standard flight check and the next morning I went to see the lady housing Captain. I explained that Colonel Gray ordered me to release Gretel because she was too young to be housed with a bachelor. The Captain asked when I was getting married.

I answered, "I'm not sure."

By the time I got home after a flight to Berlin, Gretel was gone and her replacement was already in the house, a sweet little old grandmother I called *Muti,* meaning mother. She was a professional housekeeper with a small round head and long gray hair that was braided and wrapped around her head. She smiled all the time, and sang a bit like Marlene Dietrich, doing renditions of *"Frag Nicht Warum Ich Gehe,"* "Don't Ask Why I'm Going," a sad song of lost love, and *"Mein Blondes Baby,"* about a blue-eyed girl.

We got along fine and I wasn't surprised to learn she was Gretel's grandmother. Muti also frequently laughed at my German because, in spite of a perfect accent, my choice of words was old fashioned, like *fabelhaft,* fabulous. She especially liked to walk Fritz down the street, proudly showing him off, and she loved to give him baths, during which she would sing to him and throw towels all over the kitchen floor.

Back at the squadron word got out that I had a house because of Fritz. Most pilots and navigators lived in the BOQ, either because they were bachelors or because their wives were back in the States. It was therefore decided that my house would be ideal for parties since the BOQ had strict rules and the Officers' Club was too formal; also, German girls were verboten under the "no fraternization" military laws then in effect. So the squadron took over my house, save for Colonel Gray who was not informed.

The next few days, the house suffered a transition from my private little kingdom into a clandestine speakeasy. A Major in the squadron reorganized the house and stocked it with liquor and dozens of drinking glasses. I was moved from the master bedroom to the attic, where I was to live, more like a church mouse than housemaster.

A fund was created and the proceeds were used to organize great parties, and to buy steaks for Fritz at the commissary, because his continued health was vital to the preservation of "Fritz's Party House," which was the new name given my assigned house in Zeppelinheim. Grandma, Muti, gleefully went along because, to her, these flying men were like young gods. She even asked me once, "What keeps the airplanes in the air?"

The squadron decided to make Fritz the official mascot and to start taking him on our missions around Europe and Africa. He loved the attention, and took quickly to the motion of flying, both in good and bad weather, even when strapped down to the floor of one plane or another.

We flew to Philippeville, Algeria, to teach the French Foreign Legion parachute jumping and Fritz loved the attention. Because no dogs were allowed in the regiment, he was petted by at least 200 soldiers, and the French Commandant's wife, Madame Sauvignac, wanted to keep him.

A week later we were in Lisbon, Portugal, with a Congressional delegation of Senators and Congressmen. Fritz went everywhere with Senator McClellan of Arkansas, who wanted to adopt him, too.

By this time my house was no longer really mine. Parties went on day and night. Our squadron was flying day and night, so there were officers off duty all the time. The phonograph and Armed Forces Radio blasted noisy jazz, and the lights never dimmed. Fritz moved up to the attic with me where he got as little sleep as I did.

Muti enjoyed the excitement and cleaned up willingly. She became a second mother to all the guys. She didn't seem to notice the empty liquor bottles and the constant stream of girls who flowed through the house, dancing and doing other things besides.

The majority of single officers in the squadron participated in this endless blast. There were special occasions, like the 4th of July with indoor firecrackers, and especially New Year's Eve when the greatest party of all flowed out onto the street.

I was getting to be famous, but for all the wrong reasons. Still, Fritz was our hero because he was the one responsible for acquiring the house. At one squadron bull session, one of the pilots suggested we get a parachute for Fritz. The riggers made up a small chute for him that he would never wear but we took it along anyway.

Through all this excitement my life was going down the drain. I'd lost sight of those wonderful two weeks when I was alone with Fritz and Gretel in our quiet house with our lovely little banquets. Now my world was just as noisy as when I'd had a main floor closet of a room in Jake Brodsky's bowling alley in Wiesbaden.

If I had a nice girl to take out, I couldn't invite her into this virtual house of ill repute, "Fritz's Party House." A person never knew who would show up, and with what.

It all came to an abrupt end one June day. My father cabled me that he was on his way to Europe and would be in Frankfurt in a week. He wanted to stay with me, and he wanted me to invite an old friend of his, an Army General, to dinner. He suggested I also invite Colonel Gray and Mrs. Gray.

It took hours of cleaning up and moving furniture and hiding bottles to achieve the necessary decorum. I moved back from the attic to the master bedroom; Fritz moved back to sleeping just outside Muti's room on the main floor.

Dinner with my father and his friends came off well right up until Colonel Gray took me aside. "I hear some things about wild parties here," he said. "That will stop."

Thank God!

Part 3

I was once again "Lord of the Manor" and I resumed living the life of a gentleman with his faithful dog at his side and a fine housekeeper-cook maintaining his home. The guys at the squadron were miffed about the cessation of "Fritz's Party House," but we settled for a Saturday night party with Colonel Gray's approval.

Fritz and I enjoyed a few great months of flying around Europe, Scandinavia, and North Africa. He was always able to meet attractive new dogs wherever we were and Fritz helped me meet attractive new girls in places like London and Paris. Life couldn't have been better. Fritz was worth his weight in gold.

Then "The Pilot's Law" entered my life! It states, simply: "If you're flying along and every last thing is right... watch out!" Watch out, indeed.

One gray morning, before coffee time in the squadron lounge, orders were delivered to me, assigning me to Casablanca, Morocco, to be Aide to the general commanding the Strategic Air Command base. The last line in the order stated: "Personnel will not bring household pets to Morroco. No exceptions."

So this was it. I called Jake Brodsky, but he, too, was being transferred. He called his old friend and supplier, Herr Blohm, and asked if he would take Fritz. Frau Blohm agreed and was ecstatic along with her boys. *Unser Fritzy*, our Fritz, would come to live with them. I left them my name and new address.

The parting was difficult for me, my eyes were watering. But Fritz didn't care. He was busy sniffing his new, grand estate, and getting to know his new family. I kissed him goodbye and he licked a big salty tear from my face. He then turned his back on me and I never saw him again.

A month later I received a postcard from Wiesbaden that was scratched out in childish letters. "Dear Papa," the letter began. "I miss you. Love, Fritz." At the bottom of the page was the black inkpad print of a paw.

CHAPTER **25**

Night Flight, 1950

EXHAUST FLAMES SHOT past my right elbow as the propeller turned and smoke coughed out of the engine. My instructor stepped up on the wing of the North American T-6 and whispered in my ear.

I had just completed my first nighttime check ride. I had taken off and landed in the pitch-black darkness of a moonless night at Goodfellow Air Force Base, San Angelo, Texas. I was an experienced small aircraft pilot by that point in 1950 but I had never before been at the controls of a heavy single engine aircraft at night. The exhaust fire blowing out past my arm was startling.

Captain Jack Steele, USAFR, was an angry sort of instructor and a fighter pilot who, during World War II, had mistakenly shot down an ally, a Russian fighter plane. The Russians demanded their pound of flesh but the Secretary of War stood by Captain Steele and transferred him to the Training Command.

What Captain Steele whispered to me was a continuation of a war of nerves between us, now into its fourth month.

Throughout my training he had tried in every way to shake me off. When he introduced me to acrobatics and combat flying, he started by doing snap rolls and maximum attitude dives at unusually low altitudes. He expected me to get sick or quit but I knew what he was doing and stuck with him.

I didn't tell him I had learned to fly eight years earlier when my family had a summer house in Great Barrington, Massachusetts. At Lufbery

Field, named after American Air ace, Raoul Lufbery, I'd had an instructor named Jim Scholts, a World War I Navy pilot, who trained me in a Sopwith triplane and in a Waco biplane.

My secret was almost revealed one day after a cross-country flight when we were coming in for a landing and I was a bit high, perhaps 30 feet. I "slipped" the plane to lose altitude by cross controlling, an old trick that was no longer accepted practice.

"Where did you learn that?" he asked but I didn't answer.

It was enough that I was everything Steele detested, "a smartass West Pointer who acted like the boss's son," as he often told the other instructors. He resented that I was "regular" Air Force and that he, an accomplished fighter pilot, was a reserve officer. It didn't help matters any that I drove around in a flashy convertible and popped in and out of the Officers Club with laughing girls while he sat alone at the bar.

Captain Steele stood out from the other instructors, too. His hair was black and ruffled, and defied combing. His uniform looked like his hair, unmanageable. The other officers didn't know what to make of him either; everyone knew he was an experienced pilot but he was tainted by scandal.

Those whispered words on the apron near the runway were the last I ever heard from "Captain Jack," for I would soon be moving on to Vance Air Force Base in Oklahoma to pilot T-28s and B-25s. As I taxied away to make two more solo night takeoffs, flights, and landings, all I knew was that the sky was black and there was no way to find the horizon. Stars and lights on the ground all looked the same. All I could see was the headlamps on the plane, the flames from my exhaust burning past on the left, the soft glow of my instruments, and the white and blue runway lamps. All I knew was instinct and the whispered words of Captain Steele: "Okay, now go out and kill yourself."

When I received my Air Force wings I was assigned as an instructor. It was a major compliment for one who had just graduated, and this on the advice of Captain Steele.

CHAPTER **26**

A Night in Paris with Barbara Walters, 1951

IN THE SUMMER of 1942 my parents and I, and my older brother, Rob, drove out from New York to California. We were the guests of Harry Warner, President of Warner Bros., at his house on Malibu Beach. My father was busy financing the purchase of the broadcast station, KFWB, by its general manager, Harry Maizlish, and we were along for the ride.

I was only 16-years old, but Harry Warner and Harry Maizlish treated me as an adult. They introduced me to all the stars and writers on the set of *Casablanca,* among them Howard Koch and Mark Hellinger.

Ten years later, I was an Air Force pilot stationed in Paris when I received a call from Harry Maizlish. He said that the daughter of an old friend from Boston was going to be in Paris, and would I take her out and show her Paris. The old friend was well-known nightclub owner, Lou Walters, who would arrive in two weeks with his wife and daughters, Jackie and Barbara, at *Hotel George Cinq,* the Hotel George V.

Hotel George Cinq is one of the six palace hotels in Paris. The others: The Ritz, The Plaza Athenée, The Meurice, The Crillon, and The Bristol. These are all periodically upgraded and, in my mind, lose their charm, warmth, and hospitality accordingly. Bright gold leaf, new white plaster, and brand new tapestries lack the quality of the antique.

When I arrived at the appointed time, the lobby was crowded with well-dressed Americans. It seems that my countrymen rediscovered Paris after giving this great lady a few years to fix herself up after the Nazi occupation. The George V had become their Mecca, especially for the wealthy show business crowd that used the lobby, bar, and restaurants to exhibit and shop for people of note. As Gertrude Stein said: "Paris is where Americans can discover what it is to be American."

Up in the wood-paneled elevator the little operator, dressed like a cadet, said, *"Quel etage, monsieur?"* What floor?

"Duexieme étage," I replied, second floor.

The second floor in many older French buildings is the elegant floor with the highest ceilings. Stepping from the elevator I noted light beige, wall-to-wall carpet topped by occasional Louis Quatorze hall chairs and benches covered in bright yellow silk.

I knocked on the right side of the double doors near a polished brass rectangle with the number of the suite etched on it. A minute later Barbara's mother came to the door dressed for the evening. At her right side was a small girl, Barbara's sister, dressed to accompany her parents. We introduced ourselves, and Mrs. Walters called to Barbara who came out dressed in an attractive white A-frame dress like the ones in the Christian Dior window down the cross-street at 30 Avenue Montaigne.

Barbara was lovely. Unlike most of the young women in the hotel, she was dressed and made up modestly with almost no jewelry, a simple white bag, and white shoes. Think of Judy Garland in her first movies, or Jacqueline Bouvier before she met Kennedy.

The doorman in his formal uniform, looking more distinguished than the Hotel guests, opened the door to my car for Barbara. I slid into the driver's seat, and we drove away to the nightclub Le Monseigneur for dinner.

The maitre d' pulled back the entrance curtains and revealed a large, dark room with a tall ceiling, lit by Art Deco lanterns protruding from white walls. Violins were playing as men in white tie and tails went from table to table playing music from a Franz Lehar operetta, "The Land of Smiles."

We moved to our table, following the waiter, twisting in the dark between diners, invisible except for a tiny candle on each table, each with its own miniature lampshade with tiny hanging tassels. I ordered dinner for two: Malossol Beluga Caviar, Lobster Bisque, and Grilled Squab with Mushrooms.

I was going to tell Barbara the curious story of "The Land of Smiles," but the music was continuous and loud, and soon led into some Noel Coward songs, ending with "Ziegeuner," the Gypsy song from the operetta, "Bitter Sweet." As "Zigeuner" ended, and the strolling violinists retreated to the bandstand, an announcer introduced the greatest living zigeuner, Gypsy guitarist, Django Rheinhardt.

He had grown up as a violinist in a Gypsy camp. In a fight he was thrown into a fire, and two fingers had become paralyzed. As a result he learned to play the guitar, but could only strum it and so he devised his own jazz sound and became world famous.

I was going to tell Django's story to Barbara but he led the band in a loud jazz version of "J'attendrai," and there was no chance to say even one word to her. He played wonderfully and continuously for about an hour, all through dinner.

We left Monseigneur and drove to Rue de Liege to the nightclub Le Sheherazade, made famous by Eric Maria Remarque in his novel *Arch of Triumph*, as a meeting place for Russian émigrés. Through the years it had become a landmark and was reproduced in a dozen motion pictures, beginning with *Roberta*, featuring colorful Czarist uniforms, and aristocratic waiters with elegant titles, wearing Russian military decorations. We were just in time for the floorshow.

I ordered coffee and dessert, and we watched a sword dance while the band played Khachaturian's "Sabre Dance." Then there were ballroom dancers and a Russian team doing the Kasatsky dance. I wanted to tell Barbara the story about Leo Tolstoy's Prince Kasatsky, but it was too noisy.

We were served dessert: chocolate mi-cuit, a chocolate cake with a molten center, cherry ice cream, and a Grand Marnier cherry sauce. After more dances, I asked the waiter, in Russian, for the check to show off my recently learned Russian, but he replied to me in English.

We drove back to Hotel George Cinq. I escorted Barbara up to her second floor suite and said, "Goodnight."

This wonderful woman, whose lovely voice has been heard by hundreds of millions of people all over the world, didn't say one word that whole night.

CHAPTER **27**

Destiny, 1951

"In the end the self is left unfinished, it is abandoned because of the death of its owner."

--James Salter

THIS IS THE story of two marvelous men. They may not have been famous but they were my good friends when I was a new Air Force pilot. They were both highly decorated World War II bomber commanders. At different times I flew as co-pilot with them both and during the Cold War we faced terror and sometimes death. Now, all I have of those days is a photograph and a dog tag.

In the backwater history of the Air Force in the early 1950s were the flying boxcars, C-82s, nicknamed "the flying coffins," with their twin booms and twin tails, and their veteran pilots, consigned, like the Flying Dutchman, to go endlessly from one place in the world to another. As Troop Carrier aircraft, C-82s were designed to take paratroopers, supplies, and even heavy combat vehicles and drop or deliver them, under enemy fire if necessary. But the enemy was the airplane itself. Almost always fully loaded, it couldn't maintain flight if it lost one of its two engines; it was the only twin-engine airplane in the Air Force with that failing.

These pilots were lesser characters in an Air Force cast that sported dashing fighter and bomber pilots with white scarves, leather jackets, and fur-lined boots. These transport pilots had no dramatic dogfights or bomb runs over Tokyo and Berlin. Yet life and flight was anything but tedium for the pilots of the 60th Troop Carrier Group based at Rhein Main Airbase at Frankfurt am Main in Occupied Germany after the Berlin Airlift. We were showing the Soviets that we could build up the air bridge supplying Berlin at any time they wanted to re-establish the blockade, which they threatened to do often.

When I joined the 60th I had come from Wiesbaden where I was one of the officers on the extended staff of Allied Supreme Commander, General Louris Norstad. This was to be my first operational assignment. I knew nothing.

I drove up to Frankfurt and reported to Lieutenant Colonel John W. Osborn, Group Commander of the 60th Troop Carrier Group. He was a quiet, well-groomed example of the movie star Air Corps World War II pilot-type played by Gregory Peck or Clark Gable. He had been a highly decorated B-29 Squadron Commander in the War in the Pacific. He wanted me to fly with him because I spoke most of the languages in Europe. This was important because the Group flew to countries where English was not spoken in the tower.

Col. Osborn said, "First, I am assigning you to fly with Captain Sterling Hinton. He's an experienced bomber pilot from the Pacific theater. You'll learn a lot."

Hinton was a tall, large-framed, blond man with a well-proportioned face. Women would say he was handsome. We were not equals; it was more teacher and pupil. Sitting together at the controls of our flying truck, a slow, unwieldy, rattling, ugly, hard-to-fly airplane, we shared hours in the air, often in formation, on both sunny days in the burning blue sky and through hours of nighttime thunder, lightning, cold and windy, drenching darkness. Sometimes he acted like a big brother or a camp counselor, but always he was someone I admired for the cloth of his uniforms, the way he talked, and the way he cupped his hand when he lit his cigarette with his Zippo lighter.

On the 13th of November 1951, I was scheduled to fly in one of two planes to Merignac Air Field in Bordeaux on the Atlantic Coast of France where we were building a bomber base. I was stopped at the squadron shack and told that I couldn't fly because I had already flown

14 hours in the past 24 hours, and to fly additional hours would be against regulations.

Hinton was assigned one of the C-82s with another pilot instead. The plane checked out to him crashed with all 30 people on board killed. They had been given a false altimeter setting by a local traffic controller so the plane went into the top of Mont Dore in the French Massif Central en route to Bordeaux.

I was asleep in the Bachelor Officers Quarters at Rhein Main when I received a call from Base Operations telling me of the crash and to fly to Clermont-Ferrand in central France to join a search party. Then I received a call from Hinton; he had switched planes with the pilot of the other plane and had landed safely at Bordeaux.

In Thornton Wilder's novel *The Bridge at San Luis Rey*, the author tries to understand why the particular five people were on the bridge when it fell. Was it some cosmic force or was it random chance? What was it about Captain Sterling Hinton that allowed him to board the other plane? Or, was his number up, as in John O'Hara's *Appointment in Samarra*, based on Somerset Maugham's version of the ancient tale in which a man can't escape his destiny:

> Death speaks: "There was a merchant in Baghdad who sent his servant to market to buy provisions and in a little while the servant came back, white and trembling, and said, 'Master, just now when I was in the marketplace I was jostled by a woman in the crowd and when I turned I saw it was Death that jostled me. She looked at me and made a threatening gesture; now, lend me your horse, and I will ride away from this city and avoid my fate. I will go to Samarra and there Death will not find me.' The merchant lent him his horse, and the servant mounted it, and he dug his spurs in its flanks and as fast as the horse could gallop he went. Then the merchant went down to the marketplace and he saw me [Death] standing in the crowd and he came to me and said, 'Why did you make a threatening gesture to my servant when you saw him this morning?' That was not a threatening gesture, I [Death] said, it was only a start of surprise. I

was astonished to see him in Baghdad, for I had an appointment with him tonight in Samarra."

One day we had an engine fail on takeoff at Wheelus Field in Tripoli, Libya. We were committed to the takeoff. With too little space left on the runway, Hinton shouted, "Feather number two and cut the fuel." This meant I was to turn the propellers to line up with the front to rear airstream to reduce air resistance. Because the C-82 had already started to turn sideways, pulled forward by the working left engine, we cut through the palm trees overlooking the Air Force golf club at the edge of the beach on the choppy blue Mediterranean.

Arms reached around the cockpit. The flight engineer, a master sergeant, flipped open the red covers on the overhead electrical switches and engine fire extinguishers. We regained control but couldn't maintain our 40 feet altitude because number one, the remaining good left engine, began to cough.

Hinton shouted, "Prepare for ditching [crash-landing on the water]."

I shouted into his ear, "I felt a power surge in the middle of the feathering."

"Bring back number two," he said, visualizing the situation instantly.

Surf sprayed our windshield as I restarted number two and unfeathered the propellers. Hinton fought with the controls to keep the plane upright and at the same time told me to call the tower for an emergency landing and clear all runways.

Skimming the waves, we again started to lose control when number two came back in and then coughed at full power. Hinton pulled back power halfway on both engines. They both took hold and he was able to drag the plane around to the beach at the end of the north-south runway. Damage to the landing gear required only a week of repair. It was then that I learned a great lesson from a great pilot.

The spark plugs were cracked because they had been screwed on too tight when they were changed in Athens a couple days earlier. At full power the crack in the ceramic shorted out the spark and prevented the explosion of the gas in the cylinders. By throttling back the spark no longer shorted out.

We spent the week in Tripoli while the gear was repaired. Hinton and I sailed a small boat in the bay and visited Mussolini's magnificent green marble casino that had been turned into an indoor market. We had to keep our hands in our pockets to fend off the boy pickpockets. Those were sunny, warm days with nothing to do but explore and enjoy the swarm of multitudes in the bazaars and the choice of cafes and sweet smelling restaurants.

The 60th Troop Carrier insignia was a shield with the Latin words *Termini non Existent*, "Boundaries Do Not Exist." We flew everywhere: Oslo, Norway to Tripoli in 14 hours over the Alps. Approaching those peaks was unforgettable. The snow-covered mountains rose up like a whipped cream pudding against the intense blue of the sky.

We went to Phillipeville, Algeria and taught the Foreign Legion to jump with parachutes. While there we stayed at the Hotel Poker Dice where all the chairs, windows, lamps, and decorations were in the shape of hearts, clubs, diamonds, and spades. At night in our room it was colder than in Germany. Since we'd brought no warm clothes, at around two in the morning I burned my copies of *Le Figaro* newspaper in the only place I could find, the bidet. In the morning, while cleaning up, the maid came upon the black ashes and rushed out of the room.

We flew to Constantine, the ancient Roman city south of Benghazi. We wore civilian clothes on a mission for the UN and our allies, the French colonial governments. Constantine, the deserted city of the Caesars with its high rising columns, was now abandoned to a strange enterprise: the training of prostitutes for the European market. We brought doctors and sociologists from the World Health Organization who thought they could do something to help the women. We stayed one night in a Bedouin camp. The Sheik brought us two boys, each perhaps 13-years old, and Hinton had me politely tell the Sheik that it was against our religion to have boys in our tent.

On one flight to the Gold Coast in Africa we were fully loaded and had trouble on takeoff. Nearing the end of the long black main runway at Rhein Main, we put our feet on the dashboard and pulled back together on the two control yokes. We just barely cleared some cars on the perimeter road. Then, while crossing the Sahara, Hinton broke out in a severe sweat. After a while, he was freezing. I wrapped him in a blanket and he told me he still had malaria from his time in the Pacific. He asked me not to mention the attack to anyone. I didn't.

As time went on I also flew in Col. Osborn's plane, especially on missions requiring a French, Spanish or German interpreter. One day, as we were preparing to land, the asbestos insulation around the heat exchangers caught fire. A boom leading to the tail lit up and the cockpit was filled with bits of asbestos, like tiny flying feathers, and we had to breath them. Col. Osborn landed carefully while I called the tower for fire trucks and for instructions. As we landed, the tower declared an emergency, closed the field, told us to shut down, and abandon the plane. We jumped out and got to the grass where we watched the booms melt down and the tails drop to the ground.

On April 29th 1952 Sterling Hinton and I flew to Tempelhof Airport in Berlin with a load of coal, and potatoes in great black bags moored down in our cargo compartment. The airport was old and small, and encircled with apartment houses. To land we had to drop full flaps and cut the power and go almost straight down. On the way in, Hinton said, "You have it," meaning I was to make the landing solo since he knew that I had to start relying on myself.

We loaded tremendous spools of coaxial cable manufactured in self-sustaining, but isolated, Berlin. On takeoff, I just barely cleared the top of an apartment house, lifting a wing to miss a chimney. On the way back through the Berlin Corridor we passed an Air France four-engine C-54 flying in from Marseilles. Above us, Russian MIG-15s were engaged in war exercises. Two MIGs swept past us and fired on the Air France plane, destroying two engines and injuring two passengers with 89 bullets that peppered the craft. To the Russian pilots, who have a different alphabet, the words "Air France" are similar to the words "Air Force" painted on all US planes; they were actually after us. When we landed at Marignane Airport at Marseilles one of the French ground mechanics shouted to me, "The Russians have declared war on Air France!"

In the summer of 1952, both Col. Osborn and his wife and Capt. Hinton and his wife were invited by my father to spend two weeks at his rented house at Cap d'Antibes on the French Riviera. I have a photo of them all, including my father and my sister-in-law. These were legendary days: a mixture of Somerset Maugham and Princess Grace, the south of France, clubs and beaches, yachts and evening dress at the Casinos. My father was a genial host, generous and known by every maître d' in the best restaurants up and down the Cote d'Azur.

A few months later I was moved to Paris to work in the OSI Counter-Intelligence. Before I left I had dinner with Osborn and Hinton at the Rhein Main Officers Club. It was a sober evening, sincere feelings and genuine regret at parting. Hinton gave me one of his dog tags as a remembrance.

On the 15th of May 1953, the entire Wing went up in tight formation to honor a retiring Army General. Lt. Col. John W. Osborn, USAFR, led the formation, flying his C-82. Ten miles northeast of Manheim, Germany, a USAF F-84 jet fighter suddenly shot out of a cloud and smashed into Lt. Col. Osborn's plane and bounced off into another C-82 piloted by Capt. Sterling Hinton.

In an instant they were gone.

CHAPTER **28**

The Girl with the Hazel Eyes, 1952

AS THE SUN rose in Frankfurt I had no idea that before sunset fell I would experience a horror so great that, until this moment, my mind has refused to recall the day in all its detail. The almost one thousand and one nights of our love have been erased from memory. The tenderness, the tears and joy, are lost to me. A few photographs remain but they are two-dimensional and I rarely look at them. Nor do I speak her name.

We talked together in both French and English. Her English was better than my French, though, and she laughed when I spoke words like *grenouille*, "frog," or *San Raphael*, a town we visited near Saint-Tropez in the south of France. She said that if we both lived long enough, I would become a, "Prince of the World," while she would become an old, "Madame Pipi," collecting tips for handing out towels in the men's room of a Paris nightclub.

She never wore makeup, and had no need for a bra. Her lovemaking was natural and without shame. She cursed the convent sisters who filled girls' heads with bizarre stories about men, and who had put flour or baking soda in the girls' bath water so they couldn't see themselves.

That early morning on a cold day in 1952, her head was pressed into a goose feather pillow as her hazel eyes opened slowly from a night of tenderness. She said in a low hoarse voice, "I don't want you to fly today. I've had a premonition, a terrible premonition." She threw the white duvet aside and walked across the room towards the bath. She had a way of moving her boyish body unashamedly, almost confrontationally, thrusting her little breasts and hips forward.

I replied, "I'm an Air Force pilot and I fly when I'm told to. I couldn't refuse, even if I wanted to."

She turned and looked at me. I was also nude and she studied me in a disinterested way, as though I were an El Greco painting, looking at me up and down. "Something terrible is going to happen. You cannot fly today, I beg you."

The rays of the rising sun streaked straight into the large master bedroom in the old mansion I leased in the Neu-Isenburg section of south Frankfurt-am-Main, which was not far from this US Air Force Base in occupied West Germany. I had an hour before I had to be at base operations to receive a briefing on the upcoming mission, a flight to Lourdes in Southwest France, near the Spanish border.

I shaved as we talked. Her face, which I could see mirrored behind me, was strangely transformed. Her round hazel eyes seemed too large for her face, but she had an expression I'd never before seen, a defeated look that was tragic. When I turned around, the look was gone and she smiled at me with tears forming in her eyes.

"Please, please. I will never see you again."

The house where we lived was an unusually large, pre-World War I, Alpine-style, white plaster construction with protruding dark wood beams. The owner was a formerly wealthy widow, perhaps 45 or 50, whose husband had been a Lufthansa pilot back in the 1920s. He had perished in the Second World War, flying a bomber somewhere on the Russian front. The lady lived in the house I had leased, having moved from the master suite to the guest rooms. She attempted more than friendliness, claiming affinity due to our shared relationship as a pilot and pilot's widow, but I wasn't distracted. I was obsessed with the girl with the hazel eyes.

She had seen more than any person I had ever met and she understood all she had seen. Born to a titled Belgian family, she was educated at a French convent. When World War II broke out, and the Nazis overran Belgium, her father was a head of the underground. Captured and sentenced to death by the German high command, he was sent to the south of France and she and her sister followed him by foot from Belgium, crossing battle lines to do so. She saw death, devastation, and starvation during her year of searching, and she found him, alive, in time to be freed by American troops who landed at Saint-Tropez in August 1944.

She sat on the edge of the bed while I put on my uniform. Her big hazel eyes glistened with tears. I was the ill-starred Lancelot strapping on his sword and she was the hapless Guinevere. I pulled away and looked once more into her wet eyes. At last she gave up to the inevitable, kissed me, and wiped away her tears with my finger.

On the road to the air base I thought about the coming flight. The storm clouds would be gathering over the Massif Central, the high plateau and mountains in the middle of France. Fog would cover Mont-Dore, the highest mountain, where our group lost a plane a few months before because of a faulty altimeter setting, so I remembered to check the settings carefully from three different sources.

Winds were shifting over the Massif Central and my airplane, a C-82, was a piece of substandard junk. We called the C-82 the "flying coffin" because we lost 11 out of 19 planes during my tour.

Still, I was not superstitious, although I was mindful of the morning's premonitions so I double checked the plane and tested all its controls. The radio channels checked out and the map case was in order. Our crew of four was ready. All seemed well.

There was a coughing sound and a small explosion as each engine came to life. The crew chief on the ground gave an "OK" signal with his fingers and pulled the chocks from around the tires.

Lift off was easy. The wheels came up. As we reached altitude, I milked the flaps up, set the mixture, trimmed the controls, called the tower, and got a compass heading.

We drifted under the most intense blue sky with white cotton clouds everywhere. I was tempted to leave my course and play among those clouds as I had in my earlier happy years of solo flying. Bursting through a cloud, I'd throw the plane straight down a sun shaft before pulling out and rolling over out of sheer joy. I'd yell out the open cockpit, not caring who might hear me, and become that great prehistoric bird that once ruled the earth below.

Time droned on with occasional radio chatter in several languages.

I stared out at the storybook sky. I was self satisfied and proud that I had achieved the perfect life: daily excitement in the sky and a mysterious girl with big hazel eyes to explore at night.

Suddenly, I heard my name on the radio channel I was monitoring. "Return to base. Repeat, return to base."

"Why, what's the matter?"

"Your fiancée has had a serious auto accident."

Never in my military flying experience had a mission been aborted because of a personal matter. We put the plane in a steep bank and made a 180-degree turn.

The flight back seemed endless. A painful weight descended on me and made it difficult to function. So many questions assailed me. What happened? Is she going to be all right? Is she going to die?

I remembered the year before when we drove from Germany to Paris on a gray winter day. There was a blowing rain that froze as it hit the earth and the cold sky was dark at four in the afternoon. Our car slipped on the narrow road as we entered Verdun. Her face was burning with fever. We stopped at a small hotel across from a desolate field of stones, dead trees, and mounds of earth. As I looked out of our rain-streaked room window, I was reminded of pictures of the trenches of Verdun in World War I, the barbed wire, twisted branches on stumps of dead trees, shell holes, and no signs of life.

During the night her temperature rose alarmingly. I called downstairs for help. The manager called back and said the sisters from a nearby clinic would be over soon. When they arrived they gave her a penicillin shot and I sat on a chair holding her hand. She lay still under the black cross hanging on the wall over the bed. The sisters prayed for her and then left me holding her hand until morning. When the sun rose to just barely lighten the gray sky, her big hazel eyes opened to greet me and I knew she was better.

"Was I ill?" she whispered. "Was I ill?"

Flying at 10,000 feet, I saw that the storm covering France was moving toward Frankfurt. We didn't want to be diverted to Wiesbaden so we increased airspeed by losing altitude, a violation of procedure, and disregarded air traffic control.

Just as the rain began, we made it back to Rhein-Main Airbase and landed. A jeep met us and led me to a parking pad, and to my car, outside the squadron shack at the edge of the runway. I drove to the old gothic German hospital attached to Frankfurt's Goethe University.

A doctor met me in the waiting room. "*Ihre beleibt*," he said, "Your loved one is terribly injured in the front of the head. She crashed into a truck with her small Fiat station wagon. We are doing what we can, but I have to tell you, there is not much chance she'll live."

I sat for hours in the dark waiting room. The rain reached Frankfurt and pounded the windows. The hospital seemed deserted. I felt like a boy put in a dark closet to atone for some crime, for I felt responsible for this tragic accident. What had I done to this girl? She could have found a life.

I thought about a night we'd shared in Monte Carlo. We found a room I could afford on my Air Force pay, a former maid's room at the top of the Hotel de Paris. We walked to the old casino across the square and she took some chips from me, putting several on her two lucky numbers on the roulette wheel. A few tries later, the little white ball rolled into one of those numbers and she walked out of the casino with her hands full of French francs. She gave them all to a poor Algerian woman who was sitting with a baby on a blanket on the sidewalk.

The doctor finally entered the waiting room. "*Ihre beleibt ist gestorben*," he said, "your loved one is dead. If she had lived, she would have been blind."

CHAPTER **29**

Night Blooming Jasmine, 1953

I MET HER at Rick's in Casablanca. Yes, there really was a Rick's in Casablanca, only it was called Charlie's and it wasn't as elegant as the Warner Brothers movie set. This Charlie's was owned by an ex-US Army Sergeant who stayed in French Morocco after the war. He built his restaurant and bar upstairs on the second floor of a white plaster building on the top of a hill overlooking Casablanca and the harbor looking out to the Atlantic. Most of the people sat at tables out on the long terrace, with candles and sensuous jasmine flowers in small vases on each table. The jazz music was loud.

She talked with some American Air Force officers and wore a white dress, which looked iridescent in the moonlight against her bronze skin. She was French and she couldn't speak English, so I held the trump card, as I spoke French from my days as a schoolboy in Nice. I cut into the crowd around her and offered to act as interpreter. After a little time we were alone.

I was in Morocco in the Air Force Strategic Air Command, a pilot and aide to the commanding General of the air depot, and liaison with the French Army. In spite of these exalted posts, I lived in a tent which contained three cots around a pot bellied stove, near a tent, which served as a field shower and toilet. I took every opportunity to get to a hotel or to the US Navy Air base at Port Lyauty at nearby Rabat, north of us, and only a few minutes away by plane. In the Navy, officers were treated well unlike our more egalitarian Air Force in which one couldn't invite a lady friend into a tent housing three officers.

Now, at last, I'd met a lovely French woman who deserved to be invited into a suite of rooms with a living room, not just some heart shaped bed.

It was 1953 and war raged in Korea. Brave men were dying, many of who were best friends and classmates from West Point. Why was I in Casablanca? America's strategy, at the time, was based on a theory that the North Korean attack on South Korea, which started this war, was a Soviet ploy, intended to absorb major US forces. At that point, our strategists predicted, the Soviets would commence an overwhelming attack on the free NATO countries of Europe, unleashing millions of soldiers. To counter this we established bomber bases in Morocco.

It was one of my duties, as a French speaking low ranking officer, to be liaison with the French Army and Air Force, and to attend to the Berber Sultan, Mohammed El Glaoui, when required.

The lovely young lady in the white iridescent dress, on that warm jasmine scented night at Charlie's was also part of that greater NATO plan, a small cog in the great machine. She was the daughter of a deceased French Army colonel, and was a nurse at the French Army Hospital in Casablanca. She was descended from the ancient French provincial kings, the Brabants and was widowed in the war, and had a small boy.

I asked her to lunch the next Sunday, and we met at *Les Rochées* "The Rocks." the best French restaurant on the rocky jetty, that stretched into the harbor. We had their specialty: snails in garlic and butter followed by a chicory and romaine salad with dressing made of oil, vinegar, mustard and water, prepared by the waiter at the table. Then, the main course: *Filet of Sole Veronique*, fish baked in white wine with a cream sauce and white grapes. A local wine that was sweet reflected the heat of the valleys of the snow-topped Atlas Mountains, which protect the South of Morocco. It was the kind of lunch you read about in Proust, or even F. Scott Fitzgerald, building up to romance. The burning intense blue sky, the delicious sapphire white topped ocean waves, the soft breeze, cotton puffs of clouds, and the ever present smells of mystic dishes produced by native cooks dressed in white smocks with oversized chef's white hats, with puffs at the top. Nearby played soft music from a Moroccan band, repetitive, a strange song from an Arab singer, over and over again,

She was my age or a little older, with Gallic tan skin, an aquiline nose, dark eyes, and an intense stare, the kind that forced you to tell the truth whether you wanted to or not. She had the figure of an athlete, the body of a swimmer.

As a matter of fact she was a swimmer. A member of a group who met every Sunday to swim off the coast of Casablanca on the Atlantic side, even in the icy ocean of cloudy winter days. I had been a swimmer too, but jumping into icy waters was not something I looked forward to. At lunch, she made me promise to join her polar bears the next Sunday.

She insisted that we have a cup of jasmine tea before leaving. In the Arab world, this is served with mint and crystallized rock sugar. It was intoxicating and seductive. I felt dizzy and strangely warm and in tune with my surroundings. A strong scent of jasmine: overwhelming!

Next Sunday we joined the Polar Bears. They were mostly retired French army men in old-fashioned bathing suit tops and bottoms. I jumped into the icy ocean, swam about, and became accustomed to this shocking but invigorating experience. We repeated these Sundays three more times, and followed up with lunch at Les Rochées; and completed the afternoon with the heady jasmine tea.

Finally, it was time, I believed, to consummate our friendship and budding love. She was still mourning the loss of her husband from seven years before. I had lost my love in a car crash two years before, which meant that I wasn't free of the flavor of that relationship.

We decided to go by car down to the mysterious Hotel Mamounia in Marrakech. We couldn't go to my tent at the air base, and we couldn't go to her house where her mother, an old aristocratic lady, watched over her grandchild. We certainly couldn't go to the only good hotel in Casablanca, the El Mansour, where the general manager and most of the officials knew her family.

The Mamounia, in Marrakech, was, according to Winston Churchill, "The most beautiful place on earth." That's what he told Franklin Roosevelt at the Anglo conference during World War II, when he lured

Roosevelt to Morocco to decide the strategy for retaking Europe. But, the Mamounia would not rent to anyone who did not produce identity papers or passports, and they would not take people who were unmarried and traveling together.

I devised a plan to travel with another air force officer and her, so that the three of us could check in; the two men in one room and my lady in the best ground floor suite with its own garden. I invited another staff lieutenant to drive down as my guest, and he jumped at the opportunity, not knowing of my secret plan.

We three traveled from Casablanca in my convertible with the top down. The trip took the better part of the day, passing camel caravans, and with a stop at ancient El Jadida on the southern coast for a good lunch at a French roadside café.

Approaching Marrakech on a wide boulevard lined with palms, we entered the pink stone wall separating the Mamounia from the rest of the world. There were horse drawn carriages everywhere. Donkeys and camels were led along the palm-lined drive, and red flowers were laid out in decorative patterns. The Mamounia, itself, is one of the wonders of the world. It lives in the memory of everyone who has ever been there. The public rooms downstairs are endless, with marble and patterned mosaic floors, deco furniture, and chunky wood beams. Two famous restaurants were downstairs; The French Room and another fashioned like an illustration of the Arabian Nights, with cushions for seats and turbaned waiters with slippers that turned up in the front.

We went to our rooms, showered, and came down for dinner in the exotic middle eastern restaurant. We sat on the cushions and had rosewater poured on our heads. Berber musicians played soft native music in ancient costumes, using unfamiliar stringed instruments and drums. We were fed a series of dishes from great bowls covered with cone shaped copper tops pointing four feet high. Brightly dressed tribesmen wearing baggy pants with long red sashes lifted the covers up ceremoniously. There were little cups of jasmine mint tea constantly filled by specially dressed men in white with green sashes. The food was spiced and strange and new dishes came and went. More rosewater and more music, too.

After dinner, we went to the Casino and played Baccarat. I won and then lost it all, and more. We left at midnight and returned to the Mamounia.

We went to our rooms after saying goodnight. Later, when my lieutenant roommate was sleeping, I went down the hall and gently knocked on her door. She opened, dressed in a white cotton robe, which looked more like an extended shawl. There was nothing underneath.

The rooms were the largest I'd ever seen. There was a round pool in the center of the odd shaped living room. The pool was deep and had no lip. The floor dropped into the water at an angle. The light was low, and came from sparkling little lights on the ceiling resembling stars. The walls were yellow like a sweet Rhein wine and there were prints from old Persian drawings. Strewn about were large soft hassocks in muted varying shades of beige. The wide bed stood alone, hidden from the living room only by a transparent gauze curtain. Drapes were pulled back from the open shutters of the entrance to the verandah and the private garden. The garden was surrounded with night blooming jasmine with orange trees in blossom adding sweetness to the strong perfume.

The striking, overwhelming memory was Jasmine, the intoxicating scent, supported by roses. The air was dense with this, and every breath was strong liquor. In the wooded garden, somewhere, a flute was playing a phrase over and over. We were Adam and Eve, about to bite the apple of the knowledge of good and evil.

We dropped the robes and slid into the pool. We touched each other, then climbed out and moved to the bed, which became soaked with water. The scent of Jasmine was so strong it overwhelmed the night. Trips to the warm water of the pool and to the bed continued the rest of the darkness and into the rays of dawn. Love was tender, A night to remember.

I thought of the song:

"One night of love
When hearts were young
A night to have and hold
A night to share when starlight grows old"

Victor Schertzinger/Gus Kahn

Seldom in love does everything go right, when the timing and setting conspire to turn the event into a perfect memory. A *Swan Lake* ballet to be played over and over in the mind.

It was noon and I went back to my room. My lieutenant had gone. He left a note on his bed, written on hotel stationery:

"I'm taking the train... Really!"

The next Saturday I called to make our usual date to go swim in the Atlantic. Her mother answered and said, "You are not going to see my daughter again!"

I was baffled.

She said, "We are strict Catholics, and you are not, and you are an American who comes and goes. And then there is the child."

Shortly after, I was transferred to Nashville, Tennessee, to Sewart Air Force Base for low-level attack training.

I never saw her again; but as I left, a messenger brought me a package. It contained her father's little stamp collection in an old frayed album.

Now, years later, whenever I smell the scent of jasmine, my heart thumps a little.

CHAPTER **30**

Tea with Salome, 1954

IN 1954, IN the middle of the Cold War, I flew as co-pilot on a Strategic Air Command bomber from Morocco to England. We had a bad landing at the Manston Air Base on the high chalk cliffs facing the English Channel, and there was damage to our landing gear that required several days to repair.

I got a pass and went to London, straight to 221B Baker Street, where Sherlock Holmes had lived on the third floor with Watson on the second. I had always wanted to spend a night in those rooms. The taxi driver dropped me off in the rain, at 241B Baker Street, the Sherlock Holmes Museum, where I was directed to an old bed and breakfast on the same street with a brass plaque that read: "Erected 1810."

A sallow woman in a black formless dress took an ancient key from a hook on the wall and led me up some uneven steps to a third floor room at the end of a hall with a creaky wooden floor. She opened the door to a cold dark room, handed me the key, and pointed out a steel grating on the wall.

"That, sir, is the heater," she said in a loud voice, as though she were hard of hearing. "The bathroom's at the other end of the hall near the telephone on the wall. At what time do you want your breakfast?"

"At eight," I replied and she disappeared toward the stairs.

The room had wooden beams separating walls of white plaster. Old chintz curtains with a hunting scene matched the duvet on the bed and the upholstered chair. I went straight to the heater and found that a shilling had to be put in the slot to turn on the heater. I paid the fee and went to bed.

A couple hours later I woke up shaking from cold. I put another shilling in the heater for an hour of heat but soon ran out of shillings and lay there freezing until dawn.

At eight in the morning a key turned in the door and it squeaked open. A small girl, perhaps 14, marched in, wearing a chintz dress made of material that matched the curtains in the room. She struggled with a heavy breakfast tray that held a typical, bountiful English breakfast: a large pot of tea in a quilted cozy made of the curtain material; scones; butter; marmalade; and a covered dish containing two fried eggs, a grilled tomato, a large "banger" sausage; and some sliced, pan-fried potatoes covered with bits of parsley.

I placed my ice-cold hands around the pot and wanted to hug it for warmth. The breakfast was the best I ever had.

Later, I telephoned Monte Harlip. She was a friend and a distant cousin of my father who asked me to have tea with her and an "enchanting" young lady.

I first met Monte a year before at my father's leased villa at Cap d'Antibes in the South of France. She had been a houseguest for a week and I was on leave from Paris where I had been stationed for a year.

In the 1920's and early 1930's Monte and her late husband, Dr. Gregory Harlip, owned, in Berlin, on the Kurfurstendamm, the most popular photographic studio for fashion, high society, and film photography. In 1937 they escaped the Nazi persecution of Jews and relocated to London on the fashionable New Bond Street, Mayfair. Here, they became photographers to the famous and to the royal family, sporting the coat of arms of the Duke of Kent, brother of the King.

At the Sherlock Holmes residence I brushed up my blue Air Force uniform, the only clothes I had. A traditional old black London taxi brought me to 161 New Bond Street to The Harlip Studio that was once a private house made of giant granite-block stones. There were dark blue-carpeted steps inside an arched entrance where, on the right side facing New Bond Street, there was a great square polished brass plaque on which was inscribed in large, flowing, Edwardian Bold lettering "Harlip Studios."

Monte arrived in the reception room like a doctor emerging from an operating room. Dressed in a black sweater and a black skirt, black stockings and shoes, with a double string of iridescent white pearls, she was an attractive 50-ish woman with short black hair. Her upright posture gave her an aristocratic bearing that concealed a warm kindliness as she announced to me, without formal greeting, "This is one of my greatest works."

She told the receptionist to order tea from downstairs and turned to me. "Dear boy, I have just photographed the most ravishing young woman. You will meet her as soon as she gets back into her street clothes."

We traded stories about what we each had done in the year since Cap d'Antibes, and also some incidental gossip about that week on the Mediterranean. The tea arrived, served by a well-dressed waiter from downstairs. We drank from a sterling silver tea set, with hot milk and little square sugar cubes. We ate thin toast with the crust removed and arrayed on a stylish silver rack with an elegant loop handle. Butterballs, with some initials pressed onto each half-flattened sphere, were served with jam of different colors in little silver bowls with small silver spoons in each.

Then she appeared, a light bronze, Middle Eastern beauty, thin and delicate with a face that could have been Cleopatra's, but with modest eyes cast downward. "Enchanting" was an understatement!

Her dress was a heavy black silk, and flared out from the waist in ruffles, perhaps a Balenciaga. There was a diamond broach near her left shoulder in the shape of two coconut trees with round rubies serving as coconuts and emeralds at the bottom for grass. She wore no necklace or bracelets but a single, large, diamond ring.

You don't have to be a great photographer to make this girl look ravishing, I thought, for she was dazzling and spoke in an exotic, almost English, accent.

"I live in Cairo," she said, "but I went to school in England, Cambridge, and I teach English literature." These words matched her perfect diamond broach. Quality without embellishment.

But her face, how to describe her in that moment as she sat across from me with her legs demurely crossed, sipping tea, resembling the famous painting of "Helen of Troy" by Dante Gabriel Rossetti? Her hair was almost braided, tumbling down, parted in the middle, full lips inviting a kiss, almost pouting below a sad, faraway look. Hers was the face that launched a thousand ships.

We talked while Monte served more tea and gave out little white bone china dishes with triangles of trimmed toast. I learned that her name was Dina, Dina bint 'Abdu'l-Hamid, and while we were chatting, I fantasized that she was dancing the "Dance of the Seven Veils." She twisted and turned, and showed her body in the most provocative way as she slowly stripped away the seven veils. Then she turned into Oscar Wilde's Salome, inflaming King Herod with incestuous desire.

While our small talk continued, I wondered why Monte had arranged this little tête a tête. I was close to the age of 29, and unmarried. This fact, at that time, seemed to worry older women who were self-appointed enforcers, out to match-up likely mates.

I hadn't thought of Monte as a matchmaker and suddenly looked at Dina in a different light. Could she, would she? I hardly knew her. But if she was okay with Monte, she must be a fine young lady. And her beauty, and taste in clothes and jewelry, and she teaches English literature?

I decided to speak to her literary expertise since I was a reader who liked to read an author's work in series, chronologically. We talked about how you could get immersed in the writer's mind and times, and progress through his life, experiencing both his work and his surroundings. She was enthusiastic.

Monte excused herself politely, saying she wanted to look at some prints. We talked until the late afternoon London fog seemed to enter Harlip Studio through the open salon windows. We said goodbye to Monte and went out and down the dark blue-carpeted steps to New Bond Street.

Dina turned to me. "May I give you a lift?" A long black Daimler limousine pulled up, and before I could answer we were inside and moving.

I gave the address: "221B Baker Street."

"Sherlock Holmes!" she said, and she was, for the first time that afternoon, animated and almost excited. We talked about some of the best Conan Doyle stories, especially *The Hound of the Baskervilles*.

As I stepped from of the Daimler outside my rooming house, I said, "Would you like to talk some more about books?"

"Yes I would," she said. "I'll give you my private number." She handed me her card that had just her name on it. Then she wrote her telephone number on the card using a small gold pen.

The next day, I telephoned Dina from the pay phone on the third floor of the Baker Street bed and breakfast. After several rings, she answered, and we talked for a half hour about living authors whom we had both met at some time in the past and about their books.

At last, I said, "May I take you to dinner at Prunier?" That was the best French restaurant I could think of.

"Oh," she replied. "No, no, no, no, no!"

I followed up. "Tomorrow or the next day?"

"No, no, no!"

That was that. I said goodbye and put all my coins in the payphone before I went downstairs and got more coins to call Monte.

"Monte, who is Dina, and why won't she go to dinner with me?"

"You fool," Monte replied. "Dina is going to be married to King Hussein of Jordan. I was taking her wedding pictures."

CHAPTER **31**

Hello Dali, 1955

THE WHITE-GLOVED, UNIFORMED elevator operator in the New York St. Regis Hotel pulled back the old accordion elevator gates and out strode Salvador Dali. Like Dracula, he wore an old-fashioned black velvet cape, a dark blue suit with an elegant tie and stiff white shirt, a brown vest, and a gold handled black cane. His pointed mustache was waxed and stood up like wings on some prehistoric insect. His black eyes were wide in permanent surprise because his eyebrows were high up on his face.

"Dali is hungry," he said as he walked up to me in the hotel lobby.

I was with his business manager, Mafalda Malouf Davis, a shadowy, flirtatious, Middle Eastern woman who circled around Dali with numerous business deals and promotions. She claimed to have connections to her "friend" the former King Farouk of Egypt, a self-indulgent big spender who was deposed in 1952.

It was now 1955, and Davis and I had an appointment with Dali to discuss some commercial TV spots I wanted to make using Dali to sell Lanvin Perfume products. We had already made some ads with Maurice Chevalier, and Mr. Cournand, owner of Lanvin, wanted someone who could gain his company even greater attention. I imagined the bizarre genius, Salvador Dali, saying slyly, "Promise her anything, but give her Arpege."

Dali grabbed me by the arm and reiterated, "Dali is hungry."

This business of referring to himself in the third person seemed to me a harmless affectation like the movie star, Bette Davis, playing the first Queen Elizabeth and saying, "We are not amused." Though the royal plural has a long history, this was the first time I had ever heard of an artistic genius alluding to himself as a separate object.

Dali marched into The King Cole Bar, which was connected to the hotel lobby by an open door to the left of the elevators. Our table faced Maxfield Parrish's world famous mural "Old King Cole," a masterful illustration of the nursery tale of the same name that was 30 feet long by eight feet high. Seeing the work, I thought of the old rhyme I'd learned as a boy:

Old King Cole
Was a merry old soul,
And a merry old soul was he;

He called for his pipe,
And he called for his bowl,
And he called for his fiddlers three!

And every fiddler, he had a fine fiddle,
And a very fine fiddle had he.
"Twee tweedle dee, tweedle dee," went the fiddlers.

Oh, there's none so rare
As can compare
With King Cole and his fiddlers three.

Dali pointed to the mural and said to me, ignoring Mafalda, "There is a great mystery to this painting. Dali will tell you but first you must study the mural. And we must eat. Dali is hungry."

The waiter was standing by and put a large silver bowl of cashew nuts, Dali's favorite, on the table, together with three Bloody Marys in large stem glasses, with stalks of celery sticking out. It was a drink that had been invented in the King Cole Bar and it consisted of vodka, tomato juice, and a dash of lime juice; but also salt, Worcestershire sauce, and pepper, both regular and cayenne.

"Shake it lightly," Dali said before ordering *grenouille*, or frogs' legs, although the waiter told him it wasn't on the menu. Apparently, this was a ritual expected by both men. Then Dali ordered pink grapefruit, settling for regular grapefruit, before ordering *escargot*, snails, for us all. He went on to explain that snails were slow but knowledgeable. "They are hermaphrodites," he said with a conspiratorial wink. "Dali will draw you a picture of a snail." But he didn't.

The snails arrived and we ate them from round copper trays on wooden platters using little spring-loaded grippers. I stared at the Parrish mural running on three great panels behind the bar, the width of the room. The painting showed the misty, open-air court of a stylized King Cole sitting on a stone throne, looking like the statue of Abraham Lincoln in the Washington Memorial. At the left end of the painting are the fiddlers three, and then surrounding the king are cloaked courtiers with servants bearing pipes and bowls on the right. Looking carefully, I noted that each of the court members had an annoyed look on his face and the musicians seemed dismayed, while King Cole smirked.

"I don't understand the curious expressions on the faces of all the subjects," I said but Dali didn't answer.

Our conversation then turned to business. It was an amicable meal and we agreed to meet with new proposals for an ad campaign one week later at Dali's apartment, #1610, in the St. Regis.

At the appointed time I visited the genius. After I knocked on his door, it opened a quarter way and through the gap I saw a wild animal, the ocelot, Babou, a dwarf leopard. Contrary to lore about the animal it did not bite me, although Dali was forced to squeeze through the narrow gap in the door and leave Babou at home.

We walked three blocks to 111 East 56th Street, Restaurant Laurent, where we sat down to a great lunch. Dali ordered for us: pink grapefruit, which this restaurant had, and *steak au poivre flambé au l'Armagnac*, a peppered steak drowned in Armagnac, a twice-distilled cognac, the whole dish set afire by the waiter at a side table.

While we were eating I asked Dali about the Maxfield Parrish mural and the secret behind the painting.

"Not now," he said.

I then reminded him that he'd promised to draw me a snail but had forgotten during our initial meeting.

He took one of the large folded "Restaurant Laurent" menus. On the back he quickly drew a giant snail that became a giant fancy "D" for Dali, and signed it. I still have the drawing.

When we left the restaurant, our business concluded, and our collaboration agreed to, I asked him again, while we were walking, about the Maxfield Parrish mural. "What is the secret?"

He turned and laughed, waived his cane at me, and said loudly, "The King has farted."

CHAPTER **32**

The Last of the Great Party-Givers, 1955

THE INVITATIONS WERE written like the first paragraph of an Agatha Christie story and contained absolutely no hint as to where the party was to take place, only where it was to begin: Mr. Fox's apartment in Tudor City. My parents had gone to the parties before the war and, somehow, I was on the mailing list when I got out of the army.

I can remember my parents arriving home at our apartment on Park Avenue, dressed in their evening clothes—he in white tie and tails and she in an evening gown— while we children ate breakfast after the Walker Gordon Company milkman and his horse had come and gone. They would be full of stories of a visit to an ocean liner, a dinner in the middle of Central Park, a department store taken over for part of the night, a visit to the Cotton Club in Harlem for an hour, and endless trips to exotic, unsuspected places in and near Manhattan.

Because I inherited my invitation, I began to feel that the whole party itself seemed inherited, too, from the 1920s, when it was a national duty to forget World War I and have a good time. In the post-World War II period, these ideals were old fashioned, and people were more interested in a good night's sleep than a night on the town. Still, I looked forward to my invitation each year and received it with a sense of relief at not having been left out.

Sometimes I questioned my youthful value to Mr. Fox. Whenever I did so, someone explained to me that he was always looking for attractive young people and felt safe with the offspring of former guests who had comported themselves well.

I knew that Mr. Fox worked all year on the party planning, although I recall little else about him. The most believable rumor was that he was the last surviving member of a big department store family, a bachelor whose greatest joy was in planning and executing the best party of the year, and in preserving the mystery attending such an undertaking.

As it turned out, this was the last greatest party in Mr. Fox's lengthy career as host and party planner, and the festivities commenced at 6 PM in his cluttered apartment, high over Tudor City on the far East Side of New York. My date was a young actress on Broadway who thought enough of my invitation to skip her performance that evening and join me instead.

Mr. Fox's apartment could hardly handle the great crowd of people milling around carrying overcoats, trying to converse, and balance champagne and caviar all at the same time. Downstairs, red carpets were rolled out and platoons of police with shiny boots and motorcycles cordoned off the whole street as double-decker Fifth Avenue buses pulled up from side streets.

Guests' names were checked off by several party marshals armed with clipboards while wearing official buttons and nametags.

"Did you hear we are going to New Jersey?"

"No, I think it's the Statue of Liberty."

"The Queen Mary is in town but it sails early in the morning."

We were herded into the double-decker buses and headed off into the sunset. On board each bus was a roving accordionist singing bawdy songs as we selected hors d'oeuvres.

A few minutes later we arrived at the Waldorf-Astoria on Park Avenue where a red carpet had been laid to lead us into the hotel's famous Peacock Alley where we all thought we would be spending much of the night. From there, however, the red carpet led in to the kitchen and on into a back stairway down to some railroad tracks of the New York Central Railway where a special, shiny train, puffed in wait for us on the siding. This stop of the New York Central had been used only once before, to receive President Hoover and General Pershing for a great reception honoring the hero of World War I.

The train traveled slowly as we danced onboard and tasted wine. When it finally stopped, we disembarked near the waterfront and boarded one of the large ferries that traversed the Bay of New York, the sole means of transportation between Staten Island and Manhattan before construction of the Verrazano Bridge across the Narrows. To our delight, the ferry had been transformed into one great floating dining room where we were served several excellent dinner courses.

The dishes had been removed by the time we arrived at Staten Island and we were met by hay wagons drawn up with Shire horses puffing steam into the night. We climbed onto the wagons, using bales of hay for stepping-stones, and rode to a nearby farm where square dance music was already playing as we arrived. Barbecuing was done over smoking wood and eaten between square dances, washed down by pitchers of ice cold beer.

When we returned to the ferry, desserts were laid out on the tables and coffee was being served as the ship toured the Bay of New York. It was late and in these early hours of the morning it was a thrill to pass the lighted Statue of Liberty and trace the stirring outline of Ellis Island's building while watching the fishing boats head out to the channel as ocean liners built up the necessary steam for departure.

At about four in the morning we arrived at a slip in Brooklyn and were transported by bus to the St. George Hotel. This massive, elegant hotel was the last vestige of the fading and genteel elegance of a Brooklyn of days gone by. We were ushered, by way of a familiar red carpet, through the hotel and down many marble steps to a swimming pool.

It was an Olympic-sized heated pool with beautiful ornamentation and galleries above from which to look down on the activities. We were directed into the mens' and ladies' dressing rooms and were handed bathing suits with tops for all. We were also handed lovely, giant white terry cloth robes and slippers.

A ghostly looking assemblage gathered around the pool of the St. George Hotel at 5 AM on a late Fall Saturday morning. Silently, we all understood it would have been bad form not to go into the pool.

Climbing out of the pool for the last time after swimming laps or diving from the low board, we found a buffet breakfast set up along the length of the pool on rectangular tables covered with white linen. It was a traditional English country breakfast: scrambled eggs, chicken livers on rice, bacon, kippered herring, muffins, croissants, and hot chocolate and coffee. There was a wonderfully sensual feeling to the meal, having good food after being up all night, and being half clad after a dip in warm water.

From the pool dressing rooms, our red carpet led to a train underneath the hotel that took us, with accordions and Bloody Marys, under the East River to Manhattan and to Grand Central Station at 42nd Street. Our train stopped and we climbed up the stairs and through the rotunda to emerge, incongruously, in our evening clothes at the glaring dawn of a swarming New York City morning.

CHAPTER **33**

Samuel Goldwyn, 1965

THE PHONE RANG and seemed to shake on my desk at the top floor of 625 Madison Avenue. From my office I stared out beyond Central Park as far as the George Washington Bridge with the blinding afternoon sun hanging over New Jersey. I flipped on the squawk box and heard my secretary say, "Cary Grant's business manager is on the line."

He was all business. No introductions. "Sam Goldwyn wants to see you," he said and continued on without waiting for me to answer: "He'll deliver you an American Airlines First Class round trip ticket to Los Angeles. His chauffeur and limousine will pick you up and take you to the Beverly Hills Hotel where a suite is reserved for you. The chauffeur will return the next morning at 9 AM and take you to Sam's house. You'll meet alone with Mr. Goldwyn and have lunch with him. You then will be taken to your hotel and be driven back to the airport."

Why was I getting the royal treatment?

I founded the media company, Atwood Richards Inc., in 1958, in the early days of TV when I discovered that most TV stations were in financial difficulty. They couldn't afford costly entertainment because, at the time, there was little demand for TV advertising. My newly formed agency targeted advertisers that had never used TV before, and I paid for the advertisements by providing entertainment to the stations in the form of films that I leased from Hollywood studios. A win-win situation. My company was growing daily by selling considerably discounted advertising to 160 new major advertisers, including American Airlines,

Arpege perfume by Lanvin, Manichewitz Wine, Playtex, Random House Books, Toyota, and Wella. This new business allowed me to purchase three film syndication companies that could no longer compete with me. I was at the top of my game, earning over a million dollars a year, self-made, and only 39 years old. Now I was off, I believed, to lease the best film package of them all.

Ah, but pride cometh.

I left my new home at 1155 Park Avenue and arrived at Idlewild Airport, newly renamed John F. Kennedy Airport. Those were the days when First Class passengers were hunted and harvested by the airlines, and lavished with every kind of hospitality. An angelic, uniformed, young blonde escorted me to the First Class Lounge and remained with me to serve me hors-d'oeuvres and champagne from a delicate tall stem glass. Then I followed a plush carpet right to the gate and onto the plane.

Inside the massive, four-engine, Boeing 707 "Aerojet" Fanjet the eight First Class passengers were dressed as though standing in a Saks Fifth Avenue store window. The men wore suits and ties, and the ladies hats and suits with skirts. I had a large "easy chair" seat next to the window that resembled a barber chair with a footrest. We were given a gift kit in an attractive bag containing heavy socks, toothbrush and paste, aspirin, sewing kit, pen, ear plugs, earphones, black sleeping masks, chocolate mints, and a mini blanket.

There were two First Class stewardesses. While one stowed briefcases, umbrellas, canes, and carry-ons, the other served Champagne Mimosas: one part champagne, one part orange juice served in long champagne flute glasses.

After takeoff, with my Mimosa refilled, I looked out the window, remembering New York City in the 1930s when there was only one commercial airport: Newark Airport. Some Sundays my father drove my brother, Rob, and me out to Newark to watch the airplanes take off and land. We stood at the fence at the end of the runway, and I wore my boy's leather aviator's headgear and goggles, and followed through on the landings and takeoffs as though I were the pilot of one of those early open cockpit bi-planes. "Lucky Lindy" had flown the Atlantic, and by God some day I was going to do it, too!

Now I was going off to negotiate a contract with the greatest movie producer in the world, Samuel Goldwyn, a man who was famous for saying, "A verbal contract isn't worth the paper it's written on." And: "I'll give you a definite maybe." And: "In two words: Im possible."

I knew that Samuel Goldwyn was born Szmuel Gelbfisz in Warsaw, Kingdom of Poland, Russian Empire, in 1879. At an early age he walked from Warsaw to Paris, and later went on to England. By then, he was Samuel Goldfish, a handsome young man with one great ambition, to go to America and succeed. The rest, as they say, is history.

My usual contract with film people consisted of leasing a package of movies for a given number of years for television. After much struggle and weeks of waiting to sort out terms I had previously negotiated with the Cohens at Columbia Pictures and the Warner Brothers, among others. This time, I was actually being sent for by one of the founding fathers of Hollywood, a new experience, and I had a plan to put Samuel Goldwyn Pictures on the NBC Network because I already had a relationship with NBC President Pat Weaver.

My plane landed in Los Angeles where a distinguished-looking Chauffeur, dressed in all black with shiny black boots and military-type visor cap stood in the crowd holding a printed sign with my name carefully painted in black. He went to get my luggage with my baggage receipt.

Now commenced a series of disasters that ruined my trip and undermined my self-esteem for a long time to come.

There was no luggage. Not for me. Everything was in my bag, too, my contract papers, my pills, my toilet articles, and my suit and shirt, shoes and socks, tie and belt. The Airline was duly chagrined and apologetic, and told me that if I didn't get my things back in 24 hours they would give me $200. There was no point in telling them that I needed my sleeping pills or I couldn't sleep, and I needed my good clothes to see Sam Goldwyn and negotiate a multi million-dollar motion picture syndication contract.

At the world-famous Beverly Hills Hotel the bell captain asked three times for my luggage. I explained patiently that the Airline lost my bag, and he brought me a comb, razor, toothpaste, and a toothbrush. Then

I was ushered through halls papered with gigantic green palm fronds on white background into a luxurious suite that opened onto a large rectangular swimming pool circled by green umbrellas hanging over tables and chairs.

I went to bed early but couldn't sleep. For years I hadn't slept well, all the way back to my pilot days when I regularly flew at night. My doctor had an explanation but not a cure. He said my brain was too active. Without sleeping pills there was no hope, although I vainly counted backwards from 100 at least 20 times with no result. By morning I was worn out.

Refusing breakfast, I took a cold shower and did the best I could with my clothes. The chauffeur took me to the elegant Beverly Hills Georgian estate of Samuel Goldwyn that was on a road just behind the Beverly Hills Hotel. A formally dressed majordomo was at the door and invited me in. In a few minutes, Sam Goldwyn appeared from upstairs on a circular stairway where he had entertained the greats of Hollywood, such as Clark Gable, Frank Capra, Charlie Chaplin, Bette Davis, and the legendary Cole Porter.

Goldwyn was a tall, kindly man, balding and standing erect with a slight smile. He was not at all what you'd expect from all the derisive stories and jokes and misquotes that formed his reputation. I was captivated, all the more since he treated me like a visiting mogul, an equal. He took me by the elbow. "Would you like to see my paintings?"

On his wall I recall seeing a Picasso, a Matisse, and an Utrillo. The Picasso was "Femme au chignon dans un fauteuil" (*Woman with a hair bun in a sofa*), this was a painting of Picasso's lover, Francoise Gilot, herself a famous artist. The Matisse was a still life, the almost unpronounceable "Anemones and pomegranates." And the Utrillo was not very interesting to me, just the usual street scene.

We moved through French doors to a patio that looked out to a downhill green lawn. We sat at a metal garden table with a glass top and some glasses and a pitcher with lemonade. The garden chairs were covered in upholstered flowery chintz and were most comfortable, perhaps too comfortable. I thought, *Beware of Greeks bearing gifts*.

Goldwyn turned to me. "I have chosen you to carry on my legacy by taking over all my Samuel Goldwyn pictures."

I suddenly thought of the movie, *Lost Horizon*, when the old High Lama, Father Perrault, said to the distinguished Ronald Colman, "I leave to you the future of Shangri-La." And that's how it was as we sat on the red brick terrace of what seemed like the plantation, Tara, from *Gone With The Wind*, looking past ancient magnolia trees down the green well-tended lawn.

A valet in black with a stiff white shirt and white bow tie took away our lemonade and set the table. Without explaining his, "I have chosen you to carry on my legacy," statement, Goldwyn said: "We don't talk about business at lunch." So, I had to wait to find out whether I was being offered the presidency of Samuel Goldwyn Pictures or, as I expected, a rental contract for TV broadcast rights.

Lunch proceeded. Cold fruit soup, striped fresh bass with green sauce, potatoes soufflé, French string beans with almonds, and small baguettes.

I decided to make conversation. I told Mr. Goldwyn that I'd had lunch a few days before with Adolph Zukor, founder and President of Paramount Pictures and the founding mogul of Hollywood. This was a gross exaggeration. The truth is that I had gone to the City Athletic Club for a swim followed by lunch. In the Club's dining room, where solo members shared a round table, I sat in audience to the 92-year-old Zukor. He told the diners at the table about his whirlwind Australia trip in 1916, when traveling was primitive in that part of the world. It was an interesting story, and I said to Goldwyn, "He's a nice little man. Very polite and considerate."

Goldwyn made a sound like, "Humph."

Later on I learned that when Zukor took over Famous Players and Paramount, also in 1916, he "eased out" the more flamboyant Goldwyn, a slight that hadn't been forgotten. I would never again fail to study the history of people I was to meet.

With lunch ended, we talked while the dishes were cleared. Then Goldwyn said, "I've heard you have been renting film libraries for TV from other film companies. They tell me you're the up-and-coming guy in this business. I'll get to the point: I want you to buy all the Samuel Goldwyn Pictures, worldwide rights, in perpetuity. I'll sell them as a package for $50,000 each. I'm making this special offer to you because I want you to carry on my name with honor. I know all about you; we have mutual friends. You'll have all these great pictures forever, and in every country on earth."

I did a quick calculation, and it amounted to more money than I and my company had, combined.

"These films include Academy Award winner *The Best Years of our Lives,* and Academy Award nominees *Wuthering Heights, The Little Foxes, Dodsworth, Dead End,* and *Arrowsmith*. Among the others you'll get *Guys and Dolls, The Goldwyn Follies, Hans Christian Anderson, Porgy and Bess, Hurricane, Stella Dallas, The Adventures of Marco Polo,* and *Nana*. Forever and everywhere. This will feed you and your grandchildren and their grandchildren."

I told Goldwyn that I would like very much to take him up on the deal, but that I could only pay $25,000 per picture.

He said, "No."

I told him that buying these pictures, even at $25,000, would leave me with no working capital, and that I was turning over the capital four times a year. I told him I would go back and work on it, if he would consider a better price.

"No," he said and I didn't hear from him for a year, almost to the day, when a call came in to my office.

"It's Samuel Goldwyn," my secretary announced.

I quickly picked up the phone.

"Richard," he said. "Do you remember last year you turned down $50,000 for worldwide rights in perpetuity? I just got $50,000 each picture for Canada rights alone!"

My chance at becoming a billionaire was gone, although Ted Turner later made billions with the very same plan.

Years later, when I had one of my rare heart-to-heart talks with my dying father, he said, " You never used other peoples money for leverage." I thought that my father, a great economist and banker, had paid me the highest compliment. Now, at long last, I realize this was a harsh criticism. I'd had a plan to buy up all available film libraries and rule TV by having the best content. But I didn't have the wisdom to ask for help and borrow the money necessary to make this plan a reality.

My father had always assumed that I would remember his lesson concerning borrowed money, and what Archimedes said about leverage: "Give me a lever long enough and a fulcrum on which to place it, and I shall lift the world."

CHAPTER **34**

The La Costa Story, 1965

THERE WAS A time and place, in days gone by, when grown men regained their sun-drenched childhood. They cavorted in a wonderland playground for middle aged, nouveau riche millionaires, and their escorts, in search of an elusive lost youth. The place was La Costa in Carlsbad, California in 1965. And I was there.

La Costa, now one of the most impressive resorts in the world, was conceived from the same iniquity of Sodom and Gomorrah as its parent, Las Vegas. Inspiration came from Allard Roen, who represented an organized crime syndicate headed by Moe Dalitz, the most powerful Las Vegas casino owner and racketeer. The other backers were Frank Molaskey, Mervyn Adelson, Frank Fitsimmons of the Teamsters Union, and C. Arnholt Smith, sociopathic owner of the U.S. National Bank and original financial backer of disgraced President Richard M. Nixon. In an ironic twist, this unwholesome group of partners turned a featureless seaside property, La Costa, into a world class health Mecca.

One gloriously warm and sunny fall day in 1965 I arrived at the newly-minted La Costa resort from New York with my very young, very drop-dead gorgeous, wife, Lois. We were on vacation and didn't know quite what to expect. We were processed into a small suite as swelling music blared throughout La Costa the popular song of the day:

"We'll sing in the sunshine,
We'll laugh every day,
We'll sing in the sunshine,
Then I'll be on my way"
Gale Garnett

Whenever I hear this song now, I recall La Costa in 1965, the site of my second youth, a time of wonder and joy with many happy days and nights!

Ward Hutton, the smiling boss man, showed me into the men's spa. As the sun beamed in through blowing white curtains, jolly men, completely in the nude, moved back and forth in serene comfort, going to appointments for massage, the steam room, and the sauna, or enjoying a facial, a pedicure, or herbal wrap. Then on to the center of each spa day's activity: the men's volleyball swimming pool. Here, there was laughter and loud voices, and I recognized some familiar faces serving the ball, including William Holden, star of *Sunset Boulevard*.

We were all in La Costa for a makeover, both spiritually and physically. Successful businessmen, movie stars, outstanding leaders of the Italian American and Jewish communities, golfers, tennis players, well-behaved gangsters, union bosses, gamblers, and show-business personalities from both coasts.

This scene, throughout my subsequent life, has become my idea of entering heaven. The intense light, the singing in the sunshine, the happy guys, laughter, warm water volleyball, the innocent nudity; it's the way we entered the world and the way I imagine leaving it. If this was heaven, then truly "My father's house has many mansions."

During the next 10 years Lois and I visited La Costa from New York once or twice each year. We made spa visits and rode horses around the hills before there were any private houses in view. We loved San Diego's North County so much that we decided to live there. We kept our Palomino Quarter Horses at La Costa and rode on the trails with Allard Roen, the original General Manager.

Later in our La Costa life, our broodmare gave birth to a superb colt that girls and boys would have given their right arm to own. Lois was crazy about that Palomino colt, but she wasn't alone. Roen had shown the colt to Moe Dalitz's daughter, and she had fallen in love with the little horse, too.

Soon I got a call from one of Dalitz's inner circle, Joe Mansey, "The Liquidator." He asked me if I would come over the next day and have lunch with Dalitz who wanted to buy the horse. He said it would be a great favor to him, the liquidator, if I would sell. "You know," he began, "Moe loves his daughter, Suzanne."

I was in the middle of a really tight situation. Should I sell my horse to Moe Dalitz for his sweet daughter, Suzanne, or stay loyal to my beautiful, drop-dead gorgeous wife, Lois? I remembered *The Godfather* and how the movie director failed to do a favor and cast Don Corleone's godson in one of his movies; and then awoke one morning with the severed head of his favorite stallion in bed with him.

My poor little colt!

Moe Dalitz's eyes were drilling into me, and the yellowish whites of his eyes were turning red.

Lunch with Dalitz was fraught with electricity. Mansey, "The Liquidator," was convinced I should do the right thing and make a generous gesture, and that Moe would be more than big-hearted and pay me $10,000 for a horse worth only $5,000. We were at Moe's big round table on the terrace overlooking all of La Costa. La Costa movers and shakers and Moe's lovely, very young daughter, Suzanne, sat near me.

I could see we were approaching a war of wills: irresistible force meets the immovable object. I dug in my heels: no sale. Was this going to be my undoing after all those years of flying unsafe airplanes?

There is some tragic force inside of me, looking for some challenge big enough to risk crashing and burning. During World War II in pilot training, I pictured myself flying head-on against a Nazi fighter plane pilot. I would never turn away. Come Hell or high water, I was committed to keeping my straight, head-on collision course. "Come at me you Nazi Jew-baiting bastard."

Just then Moe Dalitz addressed his daughter. "Awe, what do you want with a horse anyway? Forget it."

CHAPTER **35**

Moon Landing, 1969

THE SHIP WAS vibrating. We were pitching and rocking. It was all I could do to keep my eyes on the screen as I saw the moon approaching.

I lay on my back, looking at a small TV through the space between my feet. I gripped a railing with one hand and held a bottle of water in the other. I was in bed in our stateroom on board the MS Mermoz, a French cruise ship, in the middle of a stormy Mediterranean Sea, en route to the storied islands of ancient Greece. It was July 20, 1969, and I was watching the Apollo spacecraft, Eagle, approach the moon.

Ever since the first Neanderthal looked up to the sky a few million years ago, and saw something bright, mankind has seen the moon as a fantasy, a mystery, an object of romance and conjecture. The man in the moon, honeymoon, a lunatic, moon river, and all the rest. Now at last we were 500 feet above the surface of the moon, and landing.

Because I was born before Lindbergh crossed the Atlantic in the "Spirit of St. Louis," and because I learned to fly on an old open tri-plane before World War II, I never dreamed that in my lifetime I would see young Buz Aldrin walk on the moon. I remembered him when he was a plebe at West Point and I was an upperclassman. Just another cadet.

Now, a signal was coming in from the spacecraft to a satellite, to Houston, and from Houston to another satellite, and from that satellite to our ship, the Mermoz, down the ship's antenna into our stateroom's TV. A voice: "The eagle has landed."

Suddenly, there was a loud noise and a banging on our cabin door. Our French steward carried in a tray with a bottle of Champagne and two glasses. "Bonjour," he said. "God Bless America."

CHAPTER **36**

Hitch Your Wagon To A Star, 1980

MY MOTHER HAD big plans for me. She said I was going to be a "great man." She quoted Ralph Waldo Emerson: "Hitch your wagon to a star." She quoted Robert Browning: "A man's reach should exceed his grasp, or what's a heaven for?" She showed me the banner under her family coat of arms, which read *Supersum*, "better than all the rest."

That's heady stuff for a boy growing up. I continually tried for things beyond my reach, sometimes with success, but often with grinding failure. I always picked myself up, dusted myself off, and started all over again. Then I looked for the next, greater, challenge.

In 1980, after I sold my company to become a rancher, a promoter came to me with a flattering offer: "How would you like to be a director of INESCO, a company that has the secret to creating fusion, the basis of the formation of stars, and the ultimate source of energy, a cleaner nuclear energy for the world, lasting for years, and costing very little?"

Fusion, or the compressing and heating of hydrogen into helium, created the tiny "star" at the center of this proposition. The impressive board of directors included the world's most capable living nuclear scientist, Dr. Edward Teller, "Father of the Nuclear Bomb." Talk about hitching your wagon to a star. How about actually making a star?

I flew to New York to attend my first directors meeting in the Chrysler Building, the iconic Art Deco metal skyscraper topped with a perfect needle, below which rested modern gargoyles. The meeting was in the spectacular Board Room on the second floor, with hardwood paneling mounted diagonally to look like random rays of sunlight. In my state of wonder I had forgotten the sage words of world-renowned intellectual Groucho Marx who said, "I don't want to belong to any club that would have me as a member."

The Chairman of the Board of Directors of INESCO was a New York Congressman. He gaveled the assembled directors to order and read the minutes of the previous meeting. No objections. He then thanked us for coming and said: "I know that it is a hardship, especially because we don't have the funds, at present, to pay you directors fees."

We then moved on to the agenda and I found that I was sitting next to Edward Teller himself. The very first announcement was that I had joined the Board, and I received a hearty welcome from all members of the Board. There followed a florid, romanticized, and basically overstated, version of my biography. The chairman next explained how important fusion was for our country and for the world, and that they were looking forward to "great things" from me. Then, almost as an afterthought, he announced that I was going to be a major contributor.

Everyone clapped a polite little clap. I turned redder than usual. Struggling for words, I was saved when a secretary came in and told Dr. Teller that he was wanted on an urgent telephone call. During the break I wondered how I was going to handle the mess, knowing I had enough money for my affairs, but not enough to support a new Manhattan project.

Teller returned. "That was 'Happy' Rockefeller," he said. "She wants me to drop over to her 5th Avenue apartment after the Board meeting."

The Chairman said that the rest of us would go to the Gloucester Fish House for an early supper with the Helmsleys, owners of many of the important buildings in New York, although she, Leona, was called "Queen of Mean" because she had said, "Only the poor pay taxes."

I heard detailed plans for the super fusion machine. I didn't pay much attention because I was trying to figure out how small a donation I could make without appearing to be a penny pincher.

When the secretary, who was taking the minutes on a court reporter's dictation machine, went out to get a new tape, there was time to relax. We leaned back in plush directors' chairs and lit up cigars.

I turned to Teller. "Do you think this plan for nuclear fusion will work?"

He replied without hesitation. "Not in a million years."

"Then why are you here?"

"They pay me $40,000 a year, plus $10,000 a meeting for being on the Board."

The next day I called in my resignation.

CHAPTER **37**

Traveling Companion, 1980

I NEVER HAD such a memorable plane ride, nor did I ever make such a fool of myself. It was 1980 and I was in New York at a directors meeting of INESCO, developing nuclear fusion. After the meeting I had dinner with some celebrities at the Gloucester House before going to the Viennese Lantern on East 79th Street for a drink of sparkling Burgundy with my old Sergeant Major, Jake Brodsky. The music was great, "The Land of Smiles" by Franz Lehar, and the air was filled with zithers and violins, and schmaltzy operetta solos sung by aging Austrian opera stars.

I slept at the Hotel Fitzpatrick at 57th and Lexington and had breakfast at Bloomingdales next door. From there I took a cab to Kennedy to board an American Airlines Boeing 767-200 with a first class ticket back to San Diego, courtesy of INESCO.

First Class in those days was something special. American Airlines was happy to have you, and lavished on you the best of everything.

I sat at the seat next to the window, and turned just enough to see who was sitting next to me: a pleasant-looking, clean-shaven man in a three-piece grey suit with a clean folded white handkerchief slightly protruding the small pocket on his chest. His face was plain, neither attractive nor unattractive, very much at ease. I guessed that he was a successful accountant.

I smiled, just to acknowledge that I knew he was there, and he tipped his head slightly, as if to say, "I know that you know that I am here."

To make conversation, I inventoried, out loud and in an admiring tone, all the items on my seat, *sotto voce*: "One red white and blue lanyard with ID First Class, my name in Nameplate. One American Airlines First Class Cocktail Swizzle stick. One First Class American Airlines Amenities Kit containing," and I dumped it out, "one pair slippers, toothpaste and toothbrush, handy wipes, face cream, lipstick brush, talcum, emery board, a pair of ear plugs, and Aspirin."

His face lit up appreciatively for an instant, and he seemed to accept my little act as a winning contribution to our budding comradeship.

"FASTEN YOUR SEAT BELTS," went the loudspeaker.

"Is that for First Class, too?" I asked.

He gave no reply.

A skinny blonde attendant brought me a gift: an American Airlines mini blanket. This was followed by an offering of a tray of Champaign flute glasses containing what appeared to be orange juice, but was actually a mimosa: half champagne and half orange juice with a drop of Grand Marnier cognac, and decorated at the top with a half slice of orange. I commented to my seatmate that this drink, mimosa, had been invented at the Paris Ritz Hotel bar in 1925 in honor of Emil Zola's character, Nana. I didn't know him well enough to explain why, and he didn't ask, so we dropped the matter as all good confidantes do.

Lunch came, and a tablecloth was laid out with fine Sterling china engraved with the American Airlines insignia. We were each given heavy silverware and a crystal glass with a large, white, cloth napkin in a silver napkin ring. At a corner of the napkin was a stitched buttonhole, so that it could be buttoned onto a shirt button under the chin. Our skinny blond attendant served us preordered cheese omelets with asparagus. I mentioned to my seatmate that I was a vegetarian, to which he smiled. Then I told him why I was a vegetarian, and offered my theory of digestion and the development of the human body.

Lunch dragged on with a salad course and little hot rolls served in a silver basket wrapped in napkins. We had chocolate cake with vanilla bean ice cream and, finally, a demitasse of coffee in lovely china accompanied by little silver spoons.

I reminisced about American Airlines and told my seatmate about how I had traveled on the airline in 1940, how I once flew one of its planes, in 1944 during the war, as a copilot when I was only 18 years old. I explained how I had dinner with C.R. Smith, the former head of American Airlines, and enjoyed the company of Eddie Rickenbacker and Jimmy Doolittle all at one table. My seatmate nodded appreciatively, so I told him how I had handled advertising for American Airlines and their Americana Hotels in the 1960s, and that I created their coupon system.

The last of lunch was cleared away and the loudspeaker boomed, "PREPARE FOR ARRIVAL."

As we approached Lindbergh Field at San Diego, I noticed that my patient neighbor was carrying *The Case of Mr. Crump*, a book by Ludwig Lewisohn, which he hadn't been able to read since leaving New York. I told him I had known Lewisohn and his companion, Thelma Spear, the famous singer, and had enjoyed their company in my childhood home.

We were about to leave our seats for the exit when I introduced myself.

He said, "My name is Jonas Salk."

CHAPTER **38**

Emperor Smith, 1996

THIS IS THE story of a man who corrupted a nation. It didn't happen overnight. First he stole from his company. Then he corrupted his city, his state, and finally his country.

In 1963 I owned a Madison Avenue advertising agency that was having success promoting Las Vegas casinos and a number of other national accounts. Owners of the Sands and Flamingo told Conrad Arnholdt Smith that I could get him more national advertising for the money. He soon placed the Westgate-California tuna and dog food accounts with me.

Our first meeting was memorable. He dressed like a manikin in a 1928 Saks Fifth Avenue store window. A hand-kissing correct gentleman with the manners of an Italian Count. Tall and trim like an aging basketball player he had a tan face and the smile of a professional actor, the kind chosen to play a senator or vice-president. He usually wore a brown three-piece suit and old fashioned highly polished Buster Brown shoes.

He was also a sociopath who had no understanding of the moral difference between right and wrong. He captivated me, the way one is attracted to the mouth of a tiger. His intensity was irresistible.

I knew nothing about the corruption that Arnholdt Smith spread north from Tijuana, Mexico, through all of California. I provided discounted advertising media and my company's record drew many successful self-made men, like Arnholdt Smith. These entrepreneurs found their way to my door, ready to spend millions in order to save millions, and I gladly accepted their business. I was like a sleepwalker, oblivious to my surroundings, making little distinction between genuine business leaders and highwaymen.

Arnholdt Smith was known as "Mr. San Diego of the Century," partly because he controlled the 62-branch United States National Bank that provided money for all his ventures, both legal and illegal. He owned the Yellow Cab monopoly in California, silver mines, and the San Diego Padres baseball team. He controlled the giant public company Westgate-California, which owned hotels, massive real estate, insurance, a fishing fleet, the world's third largest tuna packers, Girard's Salad Dressing, bus lines, and California Airlines. Privately he was also financier to gangsters from New York to Kansas City, and Las Vegas to San Diego.

We did business together and times were good. I have known many charismatic, powerful men and women who couldn't stop piling up money. Eventually, they pushed too hard or didn't pay taxes, or ended in misery or death. Perhaps they never found anything of lasting value, and felt that if only they had a little more money they could make things right. They always doubled down and gambled with power and money, often power or money they didn't actually have. Finally, everyone is defeated by circumstance or time. Nobody wins.

I always came to the phone when Arnholdt Smith called. It was my fascination with his story. The haunting premonition of tragedy. In 1967 Arnholdt Smith called me at my company office. He wanted me to pay his privately owned company, Barnes-Camp, 5% of all monies paid to my company by the pet foods and tuna business of his publicly owned Westgate-California. I told him I couldn't do that because Westgate was a public company and Barnes was his personal company. I told him, "that amounts to an illegal kickback."

"Everyone does it," he said with genuine sincerity. So he went on to another company, a small competitor of my company, proposing the same kickback deal.

Many years later Arnholdt Smith told me that he'd managed to make a deal with my competitor and got the kickback. This was the money he used for an illegal political donation to the Richard Nixon for President campaign. Then he discovered that this new competitor was billing Westgate for advertising they never delivered. When he complained, they replied: "You take a little, we take a little."

In the 1980s I found myself a direct neighbor of Arnholdt Smith, in Rancho Santa Fe, California, where we both had horse ranches. We walked together several times, as neighbors do, and we talked.

Born in Walla Walla, Washington, Arnholdt Smith's family moved to San Diego when he was a boy. At age 15, in 1915, he dropped out of high school. He began working as a grocery clerk and then as a messenger for The Bank of Italy, now Bank of America. Eighteen years later, he borrowed from his older brother, Jack, and bought the small US National Bank from which he began amassing a fortune.

In 1947 California Governor Earl Warren had appointed Arnholdt Smith to the state Highway Commission and introduced him to Richard Nixon. From that point Arnholdt became the private financier of the eventual President of the United States. The relationship was complicated and by the time Nixon had been named as Vice-Presidential running mate with Eisenhower, there was a rumor that a wealthy San Diego banker had financed his nomination. This was the basis for Nixon's famous "Checkers" speech when he lied to the American public, denied his financial backing, and claimed to be penniless. Arnholdt Smith survived that controversy and wound up sitting in the Waldorf Astoria suite with Nixon the night of Nixon's election to the Presidency of the United States on Nov. 6th, 1968. There followed hundreds of crooked federal appointments.

Arnholdt Smith also created the legendary Frank Alessio, also known as "Mr. A," the "American Dream." Alessio rose up from shining Arnholdt Smith's shoes in downtown San Diego on the corner of Broadway and E Street, and became the head of Westgate and owner of Agua Caliente Race Track when it made more book than all the other California tracks combined. I can remember visiting Agua Caliente. In those days it was magnificent with restaurants, a casino, and a zoo.

Alessio also bought Hotel Del Coronado and many acres near it using Arnholdt Smith's money. With the help of Governor Pat Brown, whom they supported financially, they got the Coronado Bridge approved joining the Island of Coronado to the mainland. Ronald Reagan cut the ribbon.

Then all of this was done through a secret rider on a California bill of appropriations and against almost unanimous objection from local residents. Allesio and Arnholdt Smith's group sold the hotel and land for profits in the millions

Alessio and Arnholdt were accused of many crimes but got off because of political influence. Sometimes it was a San Diego mayor like Frank Curran or Pete Wilson, or the President of Mexico, Miguel Aleman, Governor Pat Brown, or even President Nixon.

When Alessio's hand was finally played out for income tax evasion, he was sentenced to 8 years in Federal prison. At the time, he was preparing a giant new development around Arnholdt Smith's brother's palatial ranch at San Luis Rey Downs, north of San Diego, which already had a racetrack, country club, and homes.

Following our time together as neighbors in Rancho Santa Fe I didn't hear from Arnholdt Smith again for years until he called me one day collect from prison. He had finally been convicted and sentenced for an $8.9 million bank fraud, income tax evasion, and illegal campaign contributions. He had used up his I.O.U.s from politicians, who were by then retired or dead, and, approaching 90 years of age, he was finally paying his debt to society.

On the telephone that day, Arnholdt Smith asked that I look after his daughter, Carol, who had taken over his ranch next door to mine. She was almost out of her mind at that point but I did my best to help.

More time passed and I received a call from Motel 6. Arnholdt Smith was out of prison, and out of money. He didn't have one cent. Yet when I met with him that same day he carried himself with the grandeur of a deposed Monarch.

He said that his wife, Helen, was divorcing him. When he had gone from jail to their home, he had found his clothes thrown on the steps. "Even my nice hangars had been taken out of my suits and shirts. What should I do?"

I told him to go back to his daughter, Carol. "That's where people go, to their family."

Arnholdt Smith died a few years later in 1996 in Temecula, California. He was living in a trailer with Carol.

CHAPTER **39**

Mr. Yamaguchi's Cruise, December 7, 2012

"Yesterday, upon the stair,
I met a man who wasn't there
He wasn't there again today
I wish, I wish, he'd go away."

I SAW HIM three days out from port climbing up the stairs to the Lido deck. He was a small Japanese man with big, thick, round, black glasses. He was dressed in a red shirt with gray trousers and gray suspenders. He walked bent forward a little and smiled self-consciously while carrying a white cloth bag with a drawstring.

It was November 11, 2012. We were on the magnificent luxury cruise liner, The Crystal Symphony, which caters to the 1% that doesn't care about cost. Our floating resort was passing out of the Panama Canal and entering the vast Pacific Ocean.

I wore a white terrycloth bathrobe and I was walking away from the outdoor swimming pool, alone on the deck in the early, misty morning. The small Japanese man stopped me and pointed to his white bag, and then to a white wicker table, one of many on the empty deck. He smiled an enigmatic, Cheshire cat smile, a look that was confidential, all knowing, and, most of all, conspiratorial.

I thought I had seen him before and I was fascinated as he patted his chest and pointed at himself, and said, "Yamaguchi." He pulled out a scrap of paper, and on it was the word, "Yamagishi," written in ink in shaky letters. He bowed and handed me the paper. I bowed in return and sat down at the wicker table he'd indicated.

Reaching into his white bag, he pulled out a chess box with chess pieces inside. He also carried a book on chess in Japanese. Then he pointed to me and to himself, and as we set up the chess pieces on the board I realized he spoke no English. None at all.

We started to play. He brought out his center pawns and I did likewise. We grinned at each other, as polite opponents have done for hundreds of years. A few minutes later, my defensive trap was set. I was ready for any attack. My all-powerful queen sat behind his leading pawn, threatening his position, forcing him to decide which of his important pieces he would have to lose in the event he wanted to continue.

At that point, he did the most incredible thing. He moved his pawn backwards and took my queen, a patently illegal move not allowed in any version of chess I have ever known. Nevertheless, I did not raise a question.

We played on but without my queen and, demoralized by these "new rules," I was at a decided disadvantage. Retreating to defensive positions, I eventually conceded defeat and knocked over my king in the universal signal of surrender. We stood up and bowed to each other again.

Back in my cabin, my mind began to wander. The only man I'd ever heard of with the name "Yamaguchi" was the infamous Admiral Yamaguchi, responsible for the December 7 1941 sneak attack on Pearl Harbor.

When I googled "Yamaguchi" I realized where I'd seen my chess opponent's face before. His likeness really was Japanese Vice Admiral Tamon Yamaguchi, a face that is unforgettable, and inscribed on Wikipedia with a large portrait of the Admiral wearing a Mona Lisa smile, if it was even a smile at all.

Was the little man who won at chess with a sneak attack the selfsame Admiral Yamaguchi, who, on December 7, 1941, commanded the 2nd Carrier Division, including the carriers Soryu and Hiryu, which destroyed most of our Pacific Fleet?

I looked up our ship, the Crystal Symphony. It is owned by NYK, or Nippon Yusen Kaisha, the largest and oldest Japanese shipping company with 800 ships in its fleet, with a service record that dates back to before World War II. Importantly, the ship employs a "Mr. Yamaguchi" as manager.

The next day we were at sea in the Pacific. My cabin telephone rang. It was the voice of Yamaguchi. "Palm Court," he said.

I dressed in shorts and a sweater, and went up to the deserted Palm Court on the Lido deck at the very front of the ship. Mr. Yamaguchi was seated at a wicker table with his white bag, chess set, and book of chess instructions.

Before we set up the pieces I took a pawn of his and placed my queen behind it and took the queen with his pawn going backward. Then I moved my finger sideways and said, "No, no, no," and pointed to his book of rules.

He looked it up, then looked at me, and said, "Ah."

We started to play. I decided to try to end the game as quickly as possible. I brought my queen out early and protected her with bishop and knight. After several moves I cornered his king.

He said, "Aha. Checkmate," and it was over. I had avenged the sneak attack.

Back in my cabin, after dinner, I googled Admiral Yamaguchi again. I learned that our Navy defeated him in the Battle of Midway, which decided the war in our favor. He chose to go down at night with his scuttled flagship, the Hiryu, while reciting a poem. "Let us enjoy the beauty of the moon," he said, as the Hiryu slowly sank into the Pacific, the rising sun painted on its deck. I looked up outside my cabin terrace to see a bright moon hanging in the sky.

The next day I decided to find Mr. Yamaguchi and offer to play again, this time less aggressively. I went to the Purser's desk in the ship's lobby at the foot of the giant staircase that surrounded a tall waterfall. There stood a statuesque, blonde, Scandinavian ship's officer in a crisp white uniform, her hair done in a strict bun.

"Do you have a Japanese passenger named Yamaguchi or Yamagishi?"

She went to her computer screen. After three or four minutes she looked up. "There is no Yamaguchi or Yamagishi on the ship."

I never saw the little Japanese man again.

But I still have the scrap of paper with the shaky word "Yamagishi."

CHAPTER **40**

My Doppelgänger: James Salter, 2015

ANCIENT MYTHOLOGY RAISES the question of the existence of doppelgängers, or look-alike individuals who appear and disappear mysteriously. Old Norwegian tradition has it that one may be preceded by one's doppelgänger, who shows up everywhere in advance. This tradition was perpetuated in the legendary World War II graffiti, "Kilroy Was Here," the ever-present cartoon of a bald head and nose that greeted newly arrived soldiers on liberated walls around the world.

From childhood onwards I had just such a doppelgänger. Occasionally, we would cross paths, but usually I got there just after he'd gone. His name was James Horowitz, later known as James Salter, and he was regarded as the greatest living American author at the time of his death on June 19, 2015.

Salter was born in June 1925; I was born in June 1926. He grew up on 86th Street in New York City; I grew up on 90th Street, nearby. We both went to school in Riverdale: he at the Horace Mann School, and I at the Riverdale Country School. We both graduated West Point and became pilots, and we both went through Advanced Multi-Engine Training at Vance Air Force Base. He left the Air Force in 1957, and I left in 1958. Then we both spent part of our civilian careers in the film business.

It was at school in 1941 that I first met James Salter. We boxed against each other in a tournament and he won in a mixed decision. I came out of the match with a black eye, and he with a bloody nose.

Later that day we met again at a party at 91st Street and Park Avenue. Word got around that we had pummeled each other that very afternoon, so party-goers, including J.D. Salinger and Lauren Bacall, held us in awe. In this way we discovered that there is a certain celebrity to being involved in a fight, regardless of cause or outcome.

Also in 1941, I met Antoine de Saint-Exupéry whose nostalgic writing about his early days flying the mail in South America formed the basis for all subsequent poetic writing portraying the joy of aviation. His work was so well received that it gave writers like Salter and me the courage to be emotional when describing the inner ecstasy of flight, particularly in his memoir *Wind, Sand and Stars* and the novel *Vol de Nuit* (Night Flight). The first sentence of his debut novel, *Southern Mail,* illustrates his magical touch: "A sky as pure as water bathed the stars and brought them out."

My meeting with Saint-Exupéry occurred during a lunch given by my mother for Genevieve Tabouis, the gallant editor of the French language, anti-Nazi newspaper, *Pour La Victoire*. Saint-Exupéry had served in the French Air Force and later escaped to New York to an apartment at 250 Central Park West, near the Plaza. On hiatus from military service, he became a literary phenomenon and romantic figure across North America, and a role model for me and James Salter.

In his novel *Vol de Nuit* Saint-Exupéry wrote beautifully on the subject of flying:

> "The job has its grandeurs, yes. There is the exultation of arriving safely after a storm, the joy of gliding down out of the darkness of night or tempest toward a sun-drenched Alicante or Santiago; there is the swelling sense of returning to repossess one's place in life, in the miraculous garden of earth, where are trees and women and, down by the harbor, friendly little bars. When he has throttled his engine and is banking into the airport, leaving the somber cloud masses behind, what pilot does not break into song?"

Saint-Exupéry also wrote a bit of advice on how to live well in *Wind, Sand and Stars*:

> "Il semble que la perfection soit atteinte non quand il n'y a plus rien à ajouter, mais quand il n'y a plus rien a retrancher." (Perfection is finally attained not when there is no longer anything to add, but when there is no longer anything to take away.)

In 1944, when I was learning to fly at Lufbery Field in Great Barrington, Massachusetts, Salter suddenly re-appeared in my life. He was a cadet at West Point, also learning to fly. On a cross-country night flight, in a storm, he got lost, ran out of gas, and crashed into a house. No one was hurt, and he spent the night in the house of the mayor of Great Barrington until West Point officials could come and pick him up. The catastrophe earned him, in West Point tradition, the name "Horrible Horowitz," which may have ben why he eventually changed his last name to Salter.

After a year in the Air Force, I arrived at West Point just as Salter was graduating. He went on to fly T-6s and then B-25s; I flew T-6s and B-25s when I graduated, too. I was at the annual Air Force gunnery competitions at Wheelus Air Force Base in Libya when Salter came down from Germany where he and I both flew C-82s.

Salter eventually left the Air Force in the 1950s to pursue his writing career. He landed in Hollywood where he wrote screenplays, first by adapting his books, like *The Hunters*, about jet fighter pilots in the Korean War, which was made into a film starring Robert Mitchum. As he wrote about flying in *The Hunters*, in echo of Saint-Exupéry:

> "Then it was intoxicating. The smooth takeoff, and the free feeling of having the world drop away. Soon after leaving the ground, they were crossing patches of stratus that lay in the valleys as heavy and white as glaciers. North for the first time. It was still an adventure, as exciting as love, as frightening."

By the late 1950s I had left the Air Force to establish a company in New York that syndicated the first motion pictures to be seen on television. I was constantly back and forth to negotiate contracts in Hollywood, visiting studio heads like Jack Warner, the Cohns of Columbia Pictures, and Sam Goldwyn. I was often in the same places in Hollywood as Salter was, but we didn't meet, or maybe we did, but didn't know it.

While he wrote screenplays, his own books, like *A Sport and a Pastime* and *Solo Faces*, piled up. Through these books I continued my friendship with Salter, enjoying his words and wisdom, as in this passage on the love of a child from his novel *Light Years*:

> "Of them all, it was the true love. Of them all, it was the best. That other sumptuous love which made one drunk, which one longed for, envied, believed in, that was not life. It was what life was seeking; it was a suspension of life. But to be close to a child, for whom one spent everything, whose life was protected and nourished by one's own, to have that child beside one, at peace, was the real, the deepest, the only joy."

In the same book he offers this simple passage about marriage: "Do you know what it is to be really intimate, to feel safe with someone who will never betray you, will never force you to act unlike yourself? That was what we had."

In 2012, at the age of 87, Salter published what *The New York Times* said was his greatest novel, *All That Is*. Though fictional, it nonetheless traced his life, and it was, in its essence, very much the way I saw him: like someone outside looking into the house of his life through a window. In the book he wrote: "He liked to read with the silence and the golden color of the whiskey as his companions. He liked food, people, talk, but reading was an inexhaustible pleasure. What the joys of music were to others, words on a page were to him."

In more recent years I corresponded with Salter infrequently, but I did send him my stories. He particularly liked my memoir, "Mr. Yamaguchi's Cruise," going so far as to suggest an editorial change. With light failing he still had plenty of tailwind.

On June 19, 2015, nine days after his 90th birthday, James Salter died suddenly while working out near his home on Long Island, New York. In his final book, *All That Is,* he had written an epitaph, "There comes a time when you realize that everything is a dream, and only those things preserved in writing have any possibility of being real."

www.ingramcontent.com/pod-product-compliance
Lightning Source LLC
Chambersburg PA
CBHW031836090426
42741CB00005B/266

9780578189680